Important

This volume will contribute extensively to your knowledge of the subject matter covered. However, the information contained herein is meant to be instructive only and not a substitute for professional assistance. Legal and tax decisions often depend on the particulars of an individual circumstance; therefore, seek the help of an attorney or CPA when deciding on a technical legal or tax issue.

2nd edition

Making Money on

Your Vacation

Rental Home

By Howard R. Jones, Jr.

SECOND EDITION   August 2010

PRINTING   www.Lulu.com

Jones, Howard, 1952-

    Making Money on Your Vacation Home / by Howard Jones.—2nd ed

                    p. cm.

    Includes index.

    ISBN-13: 978-0-9842654-1-1 (pbk.)

Please submit suggestions/corrections at www.VacationHomeAdvisors.com

Bulk sales are available from www.Lulu.com.

Dedication

All that I am or ever hope to be I owe to my dear mother

Table of Contents

17 Landlord Expense Deductions

Appendix

Index

Chapter Synopsis

Chapter #1 "Short Term Vacation Rentals" - Millions of people own vacation rental homes in the US and around the world. In this chapter, we will discuss the <u>payback potential for owners from renting their vacation homes</u>, including a <u>discussion of what makes short term vacation rentals unique</u>. We will then look at the wide variety of <u>rental management options</u>, and finish with an introduction to <u>owner self management</u>. When you complete this chapter, you will understand the choices that an owner has for renting their vacation home and be better prepared to make a decision as to what approach will best meet your goals.

Chapter #2 "Benefits of Owner Self Management" - For most owners getting the maximum income from their rental home is a very important objective! In this chapter, we will talk about realizing <u>big savings on property management commissions</u> and how to prepare to seamlessly transition to self management. We will also discuss "best practice" strategies for <u>increasing occupancy</u>, realizing <u>better cash flow</u> from your rentals, and your ongoing efforts to <u>lower expenses and taxes</u>. And perhaps most beneficial of all in the long run are the benefits of <u>client loyalty and retention</u>.

Chapter #3 "Getting Started with Self Management" - It will be easier, less frustrating and more financially rewarding if I can help you to get your rental management program up and running quickly. In this chapter, we cover <u>what is required of the owner</u> (that's you!) for rental self management and what kind of <u>special issues exist for your rental home.</u> We also consider <u>critical policy decisions</u> and some <u>early action plans</u> to undertake in preparing to rent your vacation home. An understanding of what is required will help you successfully begin your rental self management program.

Chapter #4 "You Don't Have to be a Computer Expert" - You don't have to be a "geek" by any means in order to successfully manage your own vacation rental home. If you are interested in undertaking an internet rental program, you're probably already familiar with, or at least willing to learn, basic computer functionality. The basics of <u>email</u>, <u>word processing</u> and <u>browsing the internet</u> are covered here, along with a brief discussion of <u>digital photography</u>. Pictures are the key when it comes to advertising your home on the internet!

Chapter #5 "Basic Hardware and Setup" - The computer setup that you have at home today is probably perfectly sufficient to run your vacation rental program. <u>Hardware requirements</u> are covered in this chapter, as well as your options for <u>internet connectivity</u>, how to ensure <u>computer privacy and protection</u>, and a few <u>computer "housekeeping"</u> chores. This is basic stuff, but preparation and planning is surely one reason you bought this book! Review of this material will help you to ensure that your system is properly setup to manage the communication and document handling requirements of a program of rental self management.

Chapter #6 "Prearranged Home Services" - Partnering with reliable service providers is as important as any responsibility you will undertake in managing your vacation rental home. Organizing an <u>effective cleaning regimen</u> and advance consideration of <u>ongoing maintenance and major repairs</u> is critical to your rental management success. This chapter will help you to know what to look for when arranging housekeeping service or when establishing partnering relationships with local vendors. Preparing in advance will help you to avoid or address the household problems and surprise expenses (not to mention aggravation) which always seem to arise at the most inopportune times!

Chapter #7 "Rental Home Setup" - There are several straightforward but important considerations in physically preparing your home for seasonal rental. We will discuss <u>setting up home access</u>, review <u>owner and guest storage</u>, share ideas for your <u>guests' safety</u>, and consider a <u>home inventory and setting up your rental home</u> with needed household items. Once your home basics are in order, your renters will more likely experience a safe, sound and functional visit, and you will have increased protection for your home and for yourself!

Chapter #8 "From Good to Great!" - Happy renters are returning renters and nothing is appreciated more by your guests than finding a comfortable home prepared in advance for their vacation enjoyment. Use your imagination and consider these suggestions to <u>increase the appeal and comfort</u> of your home. Your guests will also appreciate information and equipment that they can use to pursue <u>outdoor adventures in good weather</u> or a home stocked with books, movies and games for days when <u>indoor activities</u> are their only option. With a little foresight and effort you can do a lot to ensure a memorable guest experience!

Chapter #9 "Guest Information and Postings" - Sometimes the value that you add to your home for rental guests doesn't cost you a dime! Many of the things that you love about the area where your home is located are the same as those that your guests would enjoy. Share your knowledge! Take the time to document and leave behind for your guests <u>information on area activities</u>, <u>operating instructions</u> and <u>in-home posting</u> about the home. The more you communicate with your guests, the more likely it is that they will feel at ease, enjoy their visit and return!

Chapter #10 "Customer Service and Communication" - Customer service is certainly one of the most important aspects of a self management program and an area where a private homeowner has the power and potential to really distinguish themselves and their home. We'll discuss the importance of projecting a positive <u>customer service attitude</u> through your communications. After that we'll cover an essential step in setting up your rental home: the preparation of your <u>basic rental documents</u> i.e. lease, directions, home access instructions, etc. Let your personality shine through, and be an effective landlord at the same time!

Chapter #11 "Your Rental Home on the Internet" - Marketing is the centerpiece of your rental effort. In this chapter we will explain what <u>commercial websites</u> do, how they support your vacation home rentals and the variables that you will encounter in choosing which commercial rental websites to use. We will also address the benefits of a having a dedicated website for your home. Finally, you will <u>write your marketing text</u> by using our preformatted <u>web input sample documents</u>.

Preparing web input documents in advance will make uploading to commercial rental web sites a snap!

Chapter #12 "Time to Go Live" - This is the final step in attracting internet rental shoppers to your home! When ready, you will "go live" if you've chosen to create a dedicated web site for your home – an exciting and rewarding experience! At this point you are ready to select and populate commercial rental marketing sites using the web input documents you previously prepared. We will also explain how to create and link an online availability calendar so that potential renters only contact you for open dates, a critical and time saving exercise. After this effort is complete, your rental home will be on-line and open for business!

Chapter #13 "Reservations and Revenue" - Your relationship with your renter begins when you start taking rental reservations. Be prepared to book your guests on terms that work for everyone involved but don't put your financial goals at risk. We will walk through your options for collecting rents and security deposits, including the use of merchant credit card services. This chapter will help you to understand the fine points of collecting your rental income quickly and reliably, important in anybody's book!

Chapter #14 "Online Owner Resources" - Your internet vacation owner rental experience is made simpler by accessing online information and services, as well as online products and supplies. I'll also introduce www.VacationHomeAdvisors.com (my company) and discuss the services that we offer. In addition to online commercial rental web sites, there are many other online resources that can be an invaluable aid to owners trying to maximize the value of their rental property. We will discuss these important and time saving resources and point you to a few that we have found particularly useful.

Chapter #15 "Laws and Regulations" – Doing a little administrative research in the beginning will ensure that you are in compliance with all applicable <u>laws and licensing</u> requirements. Be aware of <u>restrictive local ordinances</u> which, in some communities, work to thwart the owner manager! We also cover <u>sales and use taxes</u> and have a discussion on several types of <u>insurance</u> that a rental homeowner should consider to protect themselves against possible risks.

Chapter #16 "Income Taxes for Rental Owners" - We discuss current federal tax law as it relates to the four different <u>ownership tax categories</u> and how this classification effects numerous deductions. We also review tax laws regarding <u>rental income</u>, including the <u>deduction of rental losses</u> against other income, and the implications for and definition of <u>personal use</u> of one's rental property. There are also opportunities to consider when <u>selling rental homes</u>, including an in-depth discussion of my <u>Combined Zero Tax Strategy</u> which may allow elimination or delay of tax when properly applied.

Chapter #17 "Landlord Expense Deductions" - If you qualify for rental business owner status, you should have a <u>basic understanding</u> of the types of and requirements for operating expenses that you may deduct from rental home income. We will start with a look at the overall requirements for <u>deducting operating expenses</u>, examine a number of commonly encountered <u>rental home operating expenses</u>, examine the basics of the <u>home office deduction</u> requirement and computation, and address the tax implications for any <u>hiring decisions</u> that an owner makes. We will also take a look at several <u>special tax situations</u> for the rental homeowner.

Appendix I - Web Input Forms

◊ General Information
◊ Bulleted Highlights
◊ Long Description
◊ Short Description
◊ Home Layout
◊ Home Amenities
◊ Specific Area Attractions
◊ General Area Activities
◊ Seasonal Rental Periods, Minimum Stays and Rates

Appendix II - Sample Rental Documents

◊ Sample Introduction Letter
◊ Sample Guest License Agreement
◊ Sample Directions
◊ Sample Home Access Detail
◊ Sample Driver Name Request
◊ Sample Credentials

Appendix III - Sample In-Home Information

◊ Sample General In-Home Information
◊ Sample Area Restaurant Information
◊ Sample Area Activities Information

Introduction

A New Opportunity for Owners of Vacation Rental Homes!

For some fortunate investors, five, ten, twenty or even fifty thousand dollars a year is not a significant amount of money. **However, thousands of short term vacation rental property owners do care about improving their returns on investment and wish to more knowledgeably participate in the management of their rental home.** For these owner investors, making money by improving cash flow from existing assets can be an exciting and welcome opportunity!

Short Term Vacation Rentals

There are hundreds of thousands of vacation homes in the United States, and millions more throughout the world. These homes range from seaside efficiencies on the coast, to modest two bedroom condominiums in golf resorts, to million dollar oceanfront 10 bedroom homes in posh resorts, to mountain villas with spectacular views, to lakefront cabins in rustic settings. *The focus of this book is on those individuals who choose to offer their vacation homes for rent for short-term visits, generally described as rentals lasting from one night to as long as 90 days.*

Vacation Renters and the Internet

Over the last ten years, millions of renters of vacation rental homes have learned to use the internet to locate the perfect vacation getaway, and these numbers continue to grow. The birth and evolution of internet based commercial rental websites showcasing thousands of homes and condos for rent has given the consumer a new and improved way to shop. From a potential renter's point of view, the ability to search out the perfect vacation location and home on their own terms and in their own timeframe, coupled with some expectation of cost saving, is overwhelmingly appealing. But this is more than just an opportunity for renters; it can also be a major boon for owners as many have discovered.

> *The advent of commercial marketing web sites in the last ten years has provided an opportunity for owners to become much more involved in the rental of their vacation homes, usually resulting in a significant increase in net rental income.*

Buyers, Owners, Landlords

Maybe you are considering the purchase of a vacation home in a resort or desirable area and are looking for guidance. Some homes make great rentals, while others don't. There are also lots of options in deciding whether and how you might rent your new home. Some owners only allow use by family and friends but are still interested in how to best handle issues like remote access and home safety, to name only a couple.

Maybe you already own a rental home and would like to get more from your rental opportunities. Perhaps you are using the services of a property management company to carry out a rental program for your home. If you are happy using a property management company, there are still many things that you can do to improve your ownership knowledge and satisfaction and the experience of your rental customers.

Many current owners have never heard of "do-it-yourself" internet rental management and have no idea of the possibilities that it presents. Other owners who are aware of the new opportunities that are available have yet to take the plunge, in many cases because they are unsure of the process and of what is involved in rental self management.

Of course, increasing numbers of rental home owners are well aware of the evolution of the vacation rental marketplace, are ready to embrace the changes and are looking for a guide book through the transition.

Regardless of how you want to handle your own vacation home, this book has something to offer you!

Self-Management of Your Rental Home

Thanks to the reach of the internet, millions now do self manage their short term rental homes in order to greatly increase rental returns, to realize enhanced control over their investment and even to achieve tax advantages.

Buying and renting your own vacation rental property can be a little overwhelming, especially in the beginning. To be successful, self-education is a must. Knowing that you have the knowledge to stay on the right track can help you gain momentum as you learn to deal with the issues involved in successfully renting your home.

I learned to manage and market my vacation rental homes at the ocean (front cover bottom right) and in the mountains (front cover top right) over a five year period, ultimately with great success. I will tell you right now that you may learn to apply best practices for your vacation rental home totally on your own, without the benefit of the lessons in this book. It may take you five years and cost you thousands of dollars in lost income, but it is certainly possible. After all, the school of hard knocks approach is the one that I took!

> *My experience shows that owners who manage their own short term rental program instead of relying on a property management company may double net income and achieve other substantial benefits.*

This book offers guidance on how to become a successful manager of your own short term rental home or condo. It is my effort at saving you the long, expensive, and difficult trials that I went through to get from frustration to fruition in vacation rental real estate.

Chapter 1

Short Term Vacation Rentals

Millions of people own vacation rental homes in the US and around the world. Some of these owners choose not to rent their homes and reserve them strictly for personal use. However, many other owners are interested in maximizing the return on their rental home and elect to rent their homes on a short-term basis to vacationers.

In this chapter, we will discuss the payback potential for owners from renting their vacation homes, including a discussion of what makes short term vacation rentals unique. We will then look at the wide variety of rental management options, and finish with a description of owner rental self-management. When you complete this chapter, you will understand the options available for renting your vacation home and be better prepared to make a decision as to what approach will best meet your goals.

- **The Payback Possibilities**
- **What is a Short Term Vacation Rental?**
- **Rental Management Options**
- **Owner Self Management**

The Payback Possibilities

Do Short Term Rentals Make Money?

As an owner of vacation rental properties in the mountains and near the ocean, I have been asked many times about my rental ownership experiences by family, friends and casual acquaintances. During my days as a consultant with "Big Accounting Firm", I made no secret of my rental homes since I was happy to rent to my coworkers. They were often quite curious about my rental ownership experience and had all sorts of questions. Naturally, working with a bunch of accountants, you might guess that the most frequent question was "Do you make money on your vacation rentals?' I feel certain that they were thinking "If this guy can make it work, I know that I can!"

I have reflected on this key question at great length. My training in accounting gave me the right tools to tackle the question, though I eventually concluded that it was not as simple and straightforward as a yes or no. In fact, my answer changed markedly over time as I gained owner experience with the opportunities and challenges of renting my vacation homes.

> *Do vacation rental homes make money? The short answer today is that it often depends on the owner.*

For instance, it depends on what you mean by making money - net annual rental income versus long term investment return as an example - plus a host of other factors. How you manage your property, what your individual tax and financial circumstances are, where your home is located, what the competition is from other rental properties, how often and for how much the home can be and is rented, how much of your own effort you put into management, what you paid for the home, what condition the home is in, whether you have a mortgage or paid cash (oh yes, many people do), etc., etc.

> **Based on my experience, one thing that I can say with absolute certainty is that I made a great deal more money and experienced much more control over expenses after I began doing my own rental management.**

What is a Short Term Vacation Rental?

If you already own your rental home, or have previously owned one, you have some idea what makes a short term vacation rental unique and what distinguishes a good vacation rental from one that's not. If you are still in the planning stage and have not yet purchased your rental home, all of your options are open. It will be especially helpful for you if we go over the basics. Keep these factors in mind as you shop!

What is the Difference between a Short Term Vacation Rental and a Long Term Rental Home?

The short-term vacation rental market is decidedly different from the long term home rental market in a number of ways, and there is very little in between. Long term rentals are seldom furnished, don't generally include utilities and are typically rented on the basis of an annual lease. Because of these factors, there is almost no opportunity for owner use.

Short term vacation rentals are the opposite. They are rented fully furnished with all utilities up and running. Renters and rental home managers communicate and establish an agreement whereby the visiting rental party uses the home for short periods, usually in conjunction with a vacation. The manager or owner is responsible for marketing the home and ensuring that the home will accommodate a worry free and enjoyable visit. Due to the desirability of homes in vacation markets and the turn key service provided, the vacation renter pays a premium price over what would be paid for a barebones long term rental. Unlike long term rentals, short term rental homes provide an exceptional opportunity for owner use.

What are the Characteristics of a Vacation Rental Home?

In managing any property to meet the needs of vacationers and short term renters, there are a number of primary distinctions. Aside from the rental term itself, short-term rentals share the following characteristics:

◊ **Desirable Location**
◊ **Fully Furnished**
◊ **Service Enhanced**
◊ **Utilities Included**
◊ **Extra Amenities**
◊ **Linens and Supplies Furnished**
◊ **Departure Cleaning**

Desirable Location

The overriding requirement for a short term vacation rental home is, guess what, location! Is it in a good vacation area? Will visitors pay a premium to stay for short periods in your home while they visit your city, town or resort? Are there sufficient amenities nearby to make the area stand out as a vacation destination? Will visitors have sufficient interest to take the trouble to plan ahead for a visit? If the answer to all of these questions is yes, then you probably have a great vacation rental home!

Fully Furnished

Although it may appear otherwise when you see the fully loaded cars arriving for the week on Saturday afternoon, vacationers are not bringing household furniture along! They will be using yours. You must provide everything they need to maximize their comfort and convenience and to fully optimize the use of your home. Sufficient seating in the living areas, adequate beds to accommodate the advertised sleeping capacity, an eating table that seats the whole gang, even outside or portable furniture to meet their needs, etc. In addition to furniture, fully furnished includes cooking and refrigeration appliances, window coverings for privacy, dishware and utensils, and the like. Many rental homes are purchased including the furnishings. Buying a home that includes existing furniture and fixtures can be a tremendous cash and effort saver for a new owner, but remember that it is the owner's responsibility to make upgrades or changes or to buy additional furnishings to satisfy rental guests.

Service Enhanced

Guests require payment guidance, questions answered, directions to the home, instructions on access, maps of the area, guidance on area attractions, home cleaning service, occasional maintenance, easy operation of appliances and electronics, and information on everything. In other words, the more you provide in the way of convenient service and anticipation of guest needs, the better they will enjoy their vacation and the more likely they will be to come back and to spread the good word about your rental home.

Utilities Included

Sometimes your guests will be arriving at odd hours – For those that do, I can guarantee you that the only thing they want to worry about is finding the light switch! A basic standard for all rental homes is that utilities must be online and performing at all times in your home. This is necessary to meet the expectations of your guests, to provide for the safety and care of your home when no one is around, and to allow for your personal enjoyment on that occasional visit.

Extra Amenities

Vacationers will give you lots of credit for a great vacation if you make a little effort to address comfort and enjoyment issues. Don't scrimp on the cable TV! Provide internet access, toys and games, movies for the kids, books for the adults, music options, etc. It also doesn't necessarily involve spending money so much as it entails making a little thoughtful effort. The things that you can do to enhance the visitors experience is limited only by your imagination!

Linens and Supplies Furnished

Most vacation rentals provide all sheets, pillowcases, towels, hand towels, washcloths, dish cloths, kitchen towels, starter soaps and detergent, starter paper products including toilet paper, kitchen towels and facial tissues. The idea is that the guest can survive at least one night or until they can make a trip to the local grocery store. This is an area where owner participation can help to optimize the quality of that which is provided while minimizing the cost.

Departure Cleaning

While some rental managers might order cleanings irregularly, or even prefer to wait to clean immediately prior to a new guest's arrival, most rental homes are cleaned right after guest departure for obvious reasons – dirty homes create problems! Trash, bugs and dirty laundry gets worse the longer it sits. Finding a good housekeeper or home cleaning service that is reliable without fail is one of the biggest challenges property managers face, but the right housekeeping resource can be an owner's best friend.

> *While it is widely thought that homes in short term rental programs suffer more abuse than those on a long term lease, many experienced owners say that just the opposite is true.*

Rapid turnover and constant vigilance by cleaning personnel is the biggest reason for this. Problems can be noted before they get out of hand and taken care of proactively. In all of the above listed dimensions, owner involvement can make the difference between an outstanding rental home or a forgettable guest rental experience.

Rental Management Options

Owners of vacation rental property now have more options than ever for managing their short term rental property including:

◊ **Traditional Property Management Companies**
◊ **Discount Property Managers (Limited Service Providers)**
◊ **Shared Management**
◊ **Internet Based Owner Self Management**

Traditional Property Management Companies

Many owners of vacation rental properties have historically used a local property management company to market, manage and care for their home. In fact, until the evolution of the internet, there were few effective alternatives, mainly due to the cost and challenges of marketing the rental home to would-be vacationers in far flung areas. Potential renters could be located anywhere in the country, or throughout the world for that matter. The individual owner had no cost efficient way to reach this potential market.

On the other hand, because they represented numerous owners, property management companies could afford to do much more national advertising, largely in magazines but also using direct mail, magazines and even billboards. Some companies also had real estate sales operations and could take advantage of another in-house resource to contact potential renters: people who had provided their contact information by expressing interest in purchasing property in the area through the sales division.

Property management companies usually have significant internal infrastructures for managing their client's rental business. This includes computer systems for tracking rentals, accounting systems for paying and accumulating expenses, administrative operations for communicating with clients and service providers, tax reporting functionality, the list goes on and on. All of these costs are passed on to the rental homeowner by way of a management commission charge, usually as a percent of rental revenue.

Management companies may charge anywhere from 20% to 50% or more of gross rents depending on a number of factors. It is also true that in some communities, rental owners are captive to a single property manager and do not have the option to manage their own property; in some of these cases, commission rates can be as high as 60%!

> *Let me make one thing clear from the outset: I am not among those who complain that all property management companies do is rip owners off.*

Management companies that coordinate all the marketing and management tasks of short term vacation rental homes and condos provide a valuable service for many home owners who are uninterested in or unable to manage their own properties. Margins in this business are often small and many professional property managers work very hard at what is often a thankless task. Like any other business, these companies are subject to varying degrees of competition and offer varying degrees of performance. Under any circumstance, however, owners must expect to pay for this professional management assistance.

Before we get into a full blown discussion of the options for owner self management, I do want to briefly discuss a couple of intermediate solutions that have cropped up for rental home management.

Discount Property Managers (Limited Service Providers)

If you decide to use a property management company, by all means negotiate for the lowest commission rate available – some companies will discuss rates, others have a one price policy for everybody. But if you are considering a discounter who offers a reduced commission in exchange for reduced effort, be cautious. You may find one who suits your circumstances perfectly, but there is a risk that you will end up paying for something that you would be better off doing yourself. Or you might find yourself doing much of the work while still paying for the service, and therefore incurring certain costs that you might have avoided.

I am not saying that a relationship with a limited service property management company will never be the answer for you. I'm just saying to be certain what you want your relationship with the provider to be, that it works for you and that you are not overpaying. My concern with limited service management is that many of the advantages of using a property management company may be lost, that no one is picking up the slack in terms of the care and marketing of the home, and that both your guest and your rental income may suffer.

Shared Management

In response to pressure from clients and the competition from commercial internet rental sites, many rental management companies are open to sharing responsibilities - and income - with you. I call this two headed management or, more specifically based on my experience, "The Two Headed Monster". I'm sure that's too harsh, but, to some extent, this is the worst of both worlds in that you may not get all the benefits but still be stuck with many of the costs. You be the judge:

The Disadvantages of Shared Management:

◊ **Marketing Costs are not Reduced Proportionally**
◊ **Competing for Reservations With Your Property Manager**
◊ **Coordination Efforts are a Pain**
◊ **Occupancy May be Compromised**

Marketing Costs are not Reduced Proportionally

First and foremost, if you as the owner are going to participate in management, then you must incur the cost of listing your rental home on the internet. While this cost is modest compared to paying management commissions, it is not going to be any less just because you are co-managing with another company. The commercial rental sites charge a fixed annual fee which does not depend on usage. In addition, you will likely still want to have your own dedicated website for your property. The development and hosting of this web site is not reduced in any way because you are sharing rental responsibilities (and commissions) with someone else. To summarize, you are sharing a substantial part of your rental income while, at the same time, realizing no savings on your marketing costs.

Competing for Reservations

When both you and your property management company are renting your home, whoever can rent it first gets the benefit! In my brief experience, the property management company and I were essentially competing for the easy bookings available during the season and I was paying them a commission for rentals which I could have easily booked myself i.e. prime rental periods in the best rental months. What is worse is that they often won the battle because they would rent my home for shorter durations than I would have settled for, especially early in the reservation season. I considered the commission I paid for these easy rental bookings to be entirely wasted.

Coordination Efforts are a Pain

You will stumble all over each other as you try to coordinate booking commitments. Let me give you an example of what I am talking about. Say someone contacts you about a possible rental. Before you can confirm availability and book the rental, you must call or email the property management company to ensure that your potential rental will not conflict with another rental that was booked by them earlier, say that morning. Then you must wait for a response, then get back with the rental inquirer to book the requested dates, then make certain that you notify the management company to note the rental dates on their schedule. All of this must be done in real time since the company may receive a call in the meantime! It soon became apparent to me that I was not willing to put up with the additional effort or delay that resulted from the need for this constant back and forth communication with the property management company.

Occupancy May Be Compromised

One of the benefits touted earlier for owner self management is the increased occupancy – In fact, I list it right after commission savings in terms of financial payback. But keep in mind that this is achieved because nobody else will manage your property as carefully as you will. No one else will take the time to carefully study the rental patterns in the area to see when it makes sense to require weekly rental minimums versus day or weekend rentals. No one else will take the time or make the effort to "fine tune" rental rates to encourage rentals during slow periods.

> *In other words, no matter how good they are or what promises they make, property managers other than yourself are just not going to be able to give your rental home the level of detailed attention and decision making that you will. After all, you own it.*

A Hard Lesson Learned – Quickly!

Let me give you an example. When I decided to try self management for the first time, I made the regrettable decision to try to "ease into it" on January 1st by sharing the rental marketing responsibilities with a management firm. In other words, I was free to rent the home myself and save the commission, but agreed to pay the management firm for those rentals that they booked. To my surprise, by January 15th they had booked a weekend in May for me. Unfortunately, this weekend booking turned out to be Memorial Day weekend! By booking the weekend early and guaranteeing themselves the easy commission, the property management company had eliminated the possibility, indeed, probability, that I could have booked the entire week for a substantially higher amount. It took me only about two weeks to get out of that arrangement.

The New Opportunity: Internet Based Owner Self-Management

Enter the internet! A new option has evolved in the last ten years for owners of short term vacation rental properties: owner self management. Why has this become an option in only the last ten years? The answer is that, prior to 1998, vacation rental home owners did not have a reliable way to market the availability and attributes of their homes effectively. Word of mouth and traditional outlets such as newspapers offered limited reach, particularly given that renters could come from far and wide. How was an owner to decide where to spend marketing dollars? In addition, these old school forms of communication did not allow for much in the way of descriptive appeal. No pictures, limited room for posting seasonal rates, etc.

Everything changed with the introduction of commercial internet rental sites. These sites, which now number in the hundreds, provided rental property home owners with access to millions of potential renters by subscribing to the service for a fixed annual fee. Because of the emergence of these internet based vacation home marketing sites in recent years, reaching potential renters is no longer a hurdle for the individual homeowner. This new internet marketing opportunity offers both challenges and benefits. Let's start with a look at what is required, before I get you all worked up about the benefits in the next chapter!

Is Self Management Right for You?

In order to check your aptitude, answer the following questions:

◊ Are you willing to trade off a little time and effort in return for increased rental income and control over your investment?

◊ Are you a proactive person who likes to deal with people?

◊ Do you take great pride in your vacation home and like to keep it "just so"?

◊ Do you enjoy creating a good rental experience for others?

◊ Are you familiar with, or at least willing to learn more about, the basics of the internet and your computer?

◊ Do you anticipate that the experience will be worthwhile and enjoyable?

If the answer to these questions is yes, you probably have what it takes to be an excellent internet landlord!

> *Assuming that you have a suitable property, I would summarize the challenges and requirements of rental self management as largely a matter of your attitude and willingness to undertake the effort.*

Chapter 2

Benefits of Owner Self Management

      In this chapter, we will talk about realizing big savings on property management commissions and how to prepare to seamlessly transition to self management. We will also discuss "best practice" strategies for increasing occupancy, realizing better cash flow from your rentals, and your ongoing efforts to lower expenses and taxes. And perhaps most beneficial of all in the long run are the benefits of client loyalty and retention. Let's examine these plus a couple of other ancillary improvement opportunities in depth.

◊ **No More Management Commissions**
◊ **It's All about Occupancy!**
◊ **Improving Cash Flow**
◊ **Lowering Expenses**
◊ **Client Loyalty and Retention**
◊ **Tax Advantages**
◊ **Home Maintenance and Condition**
◊ **Owner Control and Satisfaction**

No More Management Commissions

If you are willing to take on the responsibilities of management, you can save the management fee on every rental income dollar received. No commissions on your rental income are paid when you self manage your own rental property. This is the first benefit of self management that most vacation rental home owners look forward to and the most obvious. Let's take a look at several different management commission issues.

What do Management Companies Do?

Management companies charge a commission, or percentage of rents, in order to assist you in managing your vacation rental home or condo. In exchange for this commission, these management companies perform many of the services required to keep your home in good order and to generate rental income. This includes researching and suggesting rental rates, marketing your property, collecting rents, checking in guests, tax reporting, coordinating cleaning and maintenance services, etc. In other words, they do what they are paid to do to run your rental program.

What is a "Fair" Commission Rate?

When I owned my vacation rental homes, I paid about 30% management commission for my beach house, but that did not include cleaning. In the mountains, the going rate was 40% but that did include cleaning. You will find that property management commissions vary widely, anywhere from 15% to 50% or more of gross rents, even in a small geographic area. I can think of three main reasons for this wide variation in commission rates: 1) different services are included depending on the company, 2) the amount of competition varies and 3) new, small "mom and pop" startup companies are constantly popping up. These small startup companies often are willing to charge lower fees and to work for less in order to get established. You may also receive more personalized service - as long as they remain in business!

If the question is "what is a fair commission rate for my property management company to charge me", then the answer is "as much as the market will bear". But why worry about your rate when you can eliminate the commission altogether?

Management Company Limitations

I have stated before that management companies provide lots of help in many ways. My opinion generally of property management companies is favorable. The owners and personnel work hard and they have a lot of people to please.

Though I will be discussing a number of their limitations in the following pages, I do not mean it as criticism as much as a statement of opportunity for the rental home owner.

Management companies are facing a new challenge with the internet, primarily in terms of marketing. The key question to ask of any local property management firm is "how are you getting the word out on my rental home?" In other words, how many people do their marketing efforts reach and therefore how occupied can they keep your home?

Management companies CANNOT use the services of many of the "rental by owner" commercial web sites because they are prohibited from doing so by policy. These sites, for individuals only, charge no management fees and relatively small annual fixed fees. To be fair, there are internet opportunities for management companies to use for marketing, but they offer nowhere near the coverage afforded by the "for rent by owner" commercial websites.

With their low cost, their access to millions of visits by potential renters, their enhanced standing in search engines like Google, and their world wide accessibility, commercial rental websites have a marketing advantage that can't be matched.

Multiple Property Owners

I make no secret of the fact that owner self management benefits derive at least partly because the owner is doing some of the work normally performed by the management company. So, when a rental home is owned by multiple owners, how do you fairly decide which owner will assume the responsibility of a manager and how that individual will be compensated for their effort? First, if no owner is willing to assume property management responsibilities, then it is a moot point since self management is by definition not an option - someone has to do the work. Second, given the effort involved, some sort of payment from the non manager owners to the managing owner is reasonable to expect.

One option would be for all owners to share the responsibilities in turn, having only one manager at a time but rotating all owners through this position on a regular basis. That's fine if everybody wants to participate, but it doesn't address the issue of performance. How do you account for the fact that one owner is much more effective than another? I say do it with compensation. My suggestion is to agree on a percent of gross income to be paid to the managing owner from the other owners for each year. Why not net income? Because even some well managed rental homes only break even, especially if income is reduced for large interest payments from a loan, and the managing owner would receive nothing.

> *I suggest that you consider 10% of gross income as a starting point for possible compensation to the managing owner, and agree on more or less before the self management issue is finalized.*

When the books are summarized at year end, the compensation calculation is done and owner capital distributions or capital requests are adjusted accordingly. If a number can't be agreed on, then don't undertake the self management effort no matter how attractive the benefits. The amount of compensation is unimportant, but agreement on the amount is critical!

Management Company Contracts

The first consideration is to assess your current commitment. Do you have an active and current written contract with your property manager specifying a term of service, expiration date and the delegation of responsibilities? The better that you understand the services that are provided by your existing property management company, the better prepared you will be to rent your vacation home yourself. As I have said, I don't think it is necessary to demonize the property management industry – you're getting services for what they charge. Although you will be performing these duties once you begin to self manage, you will almost certainly be doing them in a manner much more focused on your individual home and customer relationships. *At any rate, be sure to have a copy of any existing management company contract on hand and know what it says.*

Restricted Communities

Hopefully, your property is not in a "condotel" or similar facility where you are a captive to a particular management company. If so, you may not have the choice of self management. Check your purchase contract and any bylaws to determine any constraints. If you have not purchased yet and you want to realize the benefits of self management, read all the contact fine print and ask questions of all parties to the sale to be certain that you are free to manage your new rental in any way you choose.

In addition, be sure to ask questions about your local laws and permit issues. I have included a section in this book addressing some of these issues. A few (?) localities have apparently taken steps to eliminate internet competition in support of their local property management companies and chamber of commerce members. It you have any doubts about this, just take a peek at the Chapter 15 information on possible restrictive ordinances and you will see what I mean. While I am not sure if these "restraint of trade" ordinances will survive the inevitable legal challenges, I am certain that you don't want to buy into communities where self management is going to be an uphill battle.

Billing Information

If you want to know and compare the true cost of using a property management company, and therefore the amount of potential savings for you the owner, you need to look at the payments as spelled out in your contract and as itemized on your monthly billing statement. You are probably already quite likely familiar with your monthly billing statement. I'm sure that you keep good records and copies of all statements, don't you? Adding up prior commission charges is only part of the savings. Don't forget that you will be bringing in more rents so you will pay no commission on that income either. Plus, take a look at the different types of costs that you are billed for. It is some of these costs that can be reduced through your efforts at self management.

Wind Down from Your Existing Property Manager

I have yet to hear of a management firm insisting on enforcing a termination date, but I suspect it happens. If so, then you might as well shoot for that date as your target date to fully transition to your own management program. Though it is straightforward, setting up your own rental program does take a little time and effort. If you become prepared before your contract expires, this may be a good time to try a little "comanagement". If you have to wait anyway, maybe you could benefit from the experience of shared booking responsibilities, at least until your contract expires. Just be aware of the shortcomings we discussed earlier. And be prepared to give notice to your current property management company if required to do so by your contract.

> ### *Remember, all factors considered, the ideal time to transition to 100% self management is as soon as you are ready!*

It's All about Occupancy

Occupancy is the Key to Profitability

In my experience, a major advantage of self management is a higher occupancy rate, the increased time that your property is rented. Through my control over rental rates, my personal knowledge of the property(s), the local seasons, area activities and demand for rentals, I was able to significantly increase the number of days that my properties were rented. *Aside from the management fee savings, this was the largest area of increased return that I experienced.* You may increase your occupancy by focusing thought and effort in a few major areas.

◊ **Rental Rates**

◊ **Rental Patterns**

◊ **Rental Discounts**

◊ **Maximizing Length of Stay**

Rental Rates

I generally recommend that some of your savings on property management commissions be shared with future renters by keeping your rental rates slightly below the retail rates prevailing in your area. The internet renter is looking for some reduction in cost, and you can offer a discount over your competitors, many of whom use a property management company. You do not want to sacrifice occupancy in an attempt to command higher rates. Remember that you are in a business building mode and lower initial rates will serve you better over the long run. Here are a couple of methods for arriving at starting rental rates.

- If you have rented before, you will know what your previous rate structure looked like and can work from there. You may even have a rental schedule from a prior marketing publication featuring your home. This is probably the simplest starting point for establishing a schedule that best suits your particular situation. As I said, you may even decide to reduce your rates slightly for competitive advantage. Remember, occupancy is more important that rates in achieving your income goals.

- If your home has no rental history but nearly identical properties are for rent in your area, your task is made easy simply by mimicking the published rate schedule of a competing property. This is often the preferred approach when, for instance, you own a condo in a complex with similar rental units. I suggest obtaining a rental rate schedule from an area property management company with like kind properties to have on hand for comparison purposes.

- If your home has no recent rental history and is not directly comparable to other properties, the job is slightly more difficult simply because the process will necessitate some amount of trial and error. My advice is to start the process by requesting several rental brochures from area property management companies. You may also do a little research on the internet to find the same information, but I like to have some hardcopy on hand as well. I have always found that having something to physically layout on my desk which enables me to study the competition side-by-side is an advantage. As you develop your rates, remember to keep your pricing schedule as simple and easy to understand as possible.

Start Slowly with your Rates

Keep in mind that if your property is new to the rental market then you are the new kid on the block and your rates should reflect this. After you have been in business for a while, you will get a feel for the right price point. You can always raise rates later if your home is brimming over with renters, but it's best to start slow and be too low rather than too high.

Capacity and Other Key Rental Factors

The number of people a property can accommodate is probably the single biggest point of comparison that potential renters use when doing their search, so make certain that you are clear and forthcoming about sleeping arrangements. Beyond basic sleeping capacity, there are issues of location and suitability for short term vacation rental that I refer to as "key rental factors". It is critical to make certain that you are comparing the appropriate properties by considering those rental factors that make your home different from others. Proximity to the ocean or ski slopes, condition of the home, swimming pools or Jacuzzis, all are important. The existence or lack of these appealing factors may suggest either raising or lowering your rates in order to be competitive. More on key rental factors later.

Rental Patterns

You probably have a pretty good understanding of the rental patterns in your area if you have owned your rental home for a while. A good feel as to what the different demand periods are for your property is important in order to be an effective self manager. Summer is typically an "in-demand" period in many locations because kids are out of school. Christmas can be crazy busy at the ski slopes. *Not only will you likely scale your rental rates to higher at peak times and lower at off peak times, you may change the minimum rental periods or market to a different crowd.* Let me use Myrtle Beach, SC as an example. Summer is not golf season, but is packed with family vacationers often staying a full week. Spring and fall is ideal weather for golfers in the area, so twosomes and foursomes are always looking for housing, although sometimes for a shorter duration. The ability to micromanage rates and minimum stays is a key advantage for an owner who self manages their rental home.

Shoulder Seasons

"Shoulder seasons" are time periods which hold particular advantages for self managers. These are the days, weeks, sometimes months that see less demand because it is not peak visiting time. Self managing owners can fine tune their marketing and reservation activities to leverage these traditionally slower periods. Better occupancy during shoulder seasons can really boost income.

In summary, think about what you know from any prior rentals and from your personal knowledge of the area. Take note of what other marketers are saying and doing, both locally and on the internet. Awareness of the rental patterns in your area will be a key to keeping your home as fully rented as possible.

Pattern your rental home decision making to appeal to the broadest possible audience and to year round rental activity.

Rental Discounts

Offering discounts to fill near term vacancies is one of the smartest moves available and one of those opportunities that is hard to take advantage of if you are going through a property management company. Property management companies typically have management responsibility for many rental homes, and it is not in their business model to provide last minute, individual attention. Let me share an example.

If You Want it Done Right, Do it Yourself

I had been working with an excellent property management company for some time, but was at the stage that I wanted to see more production out of my rental home. Noticing some late season full week openings, I asked the young lady that was my "client service" contact to post a discount of 30% for these open dates effective immediately. In order to check to see if my instructions had been followed, about a week later I followed up with a phone call and posed as a potential renter. You can imagine my disappointment when I was given the standard rate and no mention of a discount was made. I don't know if it was human or system error, but it didn't really matter. An opportunity had been lost.

With only a single home to monitor, the owner manager may reduce rental rates or increase online discounts to help fill open dates that otherwise may stay vacant.

> *The ability to aggressively manage your online discounts and to make frequent adjustments as necessary to maintain occupancy is a huge advantage for the self managing owner.*

Maximizing Length of Stay

Managing Minimum Stays

Establishing minimum length visits has a couple of advantages. First, you naturally want to maximize the number of nights per visitor in order to maximize income. Second, you have to go through the same administrative process of communicating, booking, collecting rents and scheduling cleaning for every renter regardless of how long they stay. And third, you want to avoid early bookings that cherry pick your best rental days. You will always have the option to respond favorably to requests for shorter stays as open dates approach.

In my opinion, property management companies are not able to fine tune their reservation systems sufficiently for individual properties to maximize the number of rental days. *The owner, on the other hand, can stipulate weekly or even monthly minimum stays early in the reservation season when inquiries begin, and relax these restrictions as open dates approach.*

Marketing Interim Days

Another variation on this opportunity for managing and maximizing renter length of stay is to try to actively rent any open days between rentals. I encourage you to keep your eyes open for those opportunities where offering a half price sale for that extra day or two in between bookings could pay off. For instance, be proactive by sending an email to renters with adjacent rental periods noting the opportunity for an extra day of vacation at a big discount. Nobody will mind, I assure you! Offer your renters a bargain and you may find rental income that would otherwise have been lost.

Always Offer a Rental Option

If an inquiry is received for dates that are already fully or partially booked, I encourage you to respond with a positive message about what IS available that might possibly meet the potential renter's needs. And while it is generally true that people who contact you about your home are fixed into a specific time frame for their visit, you never know. You can even consider offering a discount if you have open dates which are nearing or during a period in which rentals are traditionally slow. This type of negotiating flexibility is one of the real advantages of self management!

Be sure to respond promptly to all rental inquiries whether or not you have an opening if you want anything good to happen. Even if no booking comes with the present inquiry, a quick and courteous response might result in a follow-up the next year.

Improving Cash Flow

In a traditional relationship with a property management company, initial rental payments (and sometimes deposits) may be collected well in advance of the reserved rental dates. Final payment is also often due by the renter to the company at least a couple of weeks ahead of check in. After a renter departs, the property management company typically balances the books monthly and mails income checks to owners (net of expenses) within days (or sometimes weeks) after month end. As a result, owners do not receive their funds for weeks or months after they have been received by the management company.

> *When an owner chooses to self-manage their home, they may establish their own collection schedule and gain access to funds as soon as they are submitted by the renter.*

Advance Rents

My policy was to collect a 50% "advance rent" on reservations in order to guarantee the rental period requested. I did not call this a "deposit" to avoid any problems with cashing the checks or, for that matter, spending the money. We will discuss deposits more thoroughly in a later section. Property management companies are typically required to set up escrow accounts in which to keep and segregate advance rent and deposits. In the states where my rentals were located, there were no requirements for an owner of a single rental home to do this. I expect that this is the case in most states, but you need to be sure what your state requirements are.

When booking reservations, I asked that checks be mailed immediately and agreed to hold the rental period until the check arrived. This policy worked beautifully as long as the rental guest's check in was at least 30 days away. ***In this manner I was in possession of half of my rental income early, sometimes months before the rental guest arrived.***

Even if you decide to get approved for "merchant status" so that you can accept credit cards, you may consider collecting advance rent in cash and only relying on credit cards to cover any damage deposit. If you decide to put the advance rent on the credit card immediately and collect the income, you must make certain that your incoming renter is aware of this and agrees to it. We will discuss the specifics of merchant status and accepting credit cards in a later chapter.

Income Collection

The balance of rent due from incoming renters subsequent to the initial payment was always collected at least two weeks before the rental period. In this manner, I could still rent the home if the incoming renter decided to bail on me and not send the balance due. This policy allowed me access to the total rental income before the renter ever arrived. Compare this to the delay you can expect in receiving your rental income (net of commissions mind you) from a property management company and you can see the obvious cash flow advantage.

Lowering Expenses

The more involved an owner is in their property, the more the opportunities for saving money become apparent. It is likely that nobody worries about spending your money as much as you do. I often fretted about giving a "blank check" to the management company, and found myself frustrated on more than one occasion when I was billed for something that I felt was overpriced or, worse yet, totally unnecessary. *If you are involved on a regular basis with your home, you are likely to make better decisions regarding vendor selection, obtaining bids, repairing versus replacing, etc.*

Departure Cleaning Cost

While I devote considerable space in a later chapter to hiring your housekeeper, I want to emphasize that there is a clear opportunity to save money for either you or your guests (or both) when you arrange cleaning services yourself. If you already own a vacation rental home, you were probably shocked when you first learned how much you were going to be charged by your management company for what is called a "departure cleaning". Although it is never going to be cheap to have your home cleaned after your guests leave, it is not surprising that the charges go up the more people that are between the owner of the rental home and the person actually doing the cleaning! A traditional arrangement includes a profit for the property management company as well as the cleaning service company, in addition to the basic cost of the cleaning itself. Therefore, when you as a self manager arrange for your cleaning directly there is often a significant cost savings opportunity with no reduction in service.

Cost of Supplies

Another area of potential cost savings is with the purchase of supplies for the home. If you rely on the services of an outside entity, usually a management company, to purchase and pay for supplies or needed replacements for such things as lamps, light bulbs, air filters, utensils or a host of other miscellaneous items, you will often pay full retail cost plus a markup. While some companies will take the time and make the effort to purchase prudently, others will not. There were many times that I was disappointed when I reviewed my bill and found that I was being charged for items that I had not approved at rates that I felt were excessive. If, on the other hand, you make these purchases yourself, you can shop around for the best prices and you will pay no mark up.

Choice of Premium Amenities

Although every area is unique, it is often the case that resort amenities are available in whole or in part only with payment of annual fees. When you manage your home yourself, or even if you use a property management company, you might have to decide if the additional cost is worth it for your rental home. Of course, it is not only the amenities themselves and your personal preference for these amenities that you must consider; it is what is required by your rental program that is most important.

For instance, you may consider it to be a waste of money to pay $1000 every year to have access to a community pool when your rental home is located within a block of the ocean. But if potential renters always choose your neighbor's home over yours because they want a pool, you might have to "take the plunge" financially (sorry, I couldn't resist). On the other hand, there are circumstances where it doesn't make sense to pay for amenities. Let me give you an example:

Maybe You Don't Need Every Possible Amenity

The association that was responsible for our greater beachside community charged $2000 per year for access to two community pools, use of the tennis courts, and access to certain other minor facilities and discounts. However, my little neighborhood within the larger community had a separate access right to one of the best pools on the list anyway, so it was not in my opinion necessary for me to pay the access fee for the other benefits. I know that I lost a couple of rentals over the years to tennis groups but I never felt like my rental program suffered.

Be sure that you include specific information in your marketing materials about any resort amenity limitations. You have a right NOT to purchase everything that might be available, but your potential guests certainly have a right to know what they are or are not entitled to with their rental!

Purchasing Club Memberships

Similar to the above discussion on premium amenities, you may choose to purchase retail club memberships in the greater area in which your rental home is located. Tanning salons, gyms, workout facilities and other recreational type businesses will be anxious to sell you a "discount" membership. If it adds to your rental program success, buy it. If it doesn't, don't buy it. Of course, be certain that you understand the club policy on use by non family members (your guests). Either way, always provide accurate information to your guests as to what their access opportunities are if you choose to include these private facilities in your marketing material.

Damage Waiver Fees

Charging for a "damage waiver" is the newest revenue raiser in the property management bag of tricks. You can tell from my earlier comments that I am generally a supporter of the property management industry, but I don't like the damage waiver. This is a mandatory charge that is not included in the advertised cost of the rental, but is charged to the renting consumer by management companies upon check in so that the renter "will not be responsible for accidental damages" to the home or its contents.

The reality is that damage waiver fees are almost entirely a profit center for the management company since the vast majority of the collected funds go straight to the bottom line. In my experience, very little is paid out to reimburse the owner for any damages.

It was not uncommon for me to spot a charge on my monthly billing for, say, a replacement lamp which, after much discussion, was or was not reversed and paid for through the damage waiver fund. I have never billed any such "surprise" fee to my guests and I am not aware of any owner who does, though there are bound to be a few. While nickel and dime fees have become the new reality with business in general, you can spare your guests this somewhat sneaky billing and make up for "lost" income in your advertised rate.

Purchase Warranties

Another racket...er, sorry, I meant to say, opportunity for you to spend money is a "purchase warranty". This is where you pay an amount in advance and are guaranteed repair or replacement under certain circumstance if the product fails. If someone else is in charge of your buying decisions, they may think they're a good idea for your home. I'm not THAT against buying product warranties except to say:

◊ They typically only cover the first two or three years on new products (of course, the first year is usually under warranty anyway.)

◊ It is a widely understood fact that warranties are very profitable for the companies that offer them and therefore aren't on average cost effective for the buyer.

◊ Many of them specifically exclude commercial use and that definition usually includes rental usage.

Ok, so maybe I am against them.

> **My perspective is that if I am not buying a product that will last me for at least a few years without breaking, I am probably buying the wrong product.**

In the past, I've noticed that when I've shared that perspective with a salesman, they usually don't mention purchasing the warranty again!

Client Loyalty and Retention

Client loyalty is almost non existent when an owner uses a property management company to manage their vacation rental home. I don't mean this as a criticism of any kind, but rather as a statement of fact that results from the understandable disconnect between the owner of the home and the renter. Once you as the owner begin communicating with your renters (and potential renters), you will be surprised how quickly a good relationship can be built. **And when a renter has a relaxing and enjoyable rental experience in your home, their loyalty can pay important and increasing dividends over time.**

Repeat Renters

Repeat renters are the golden goose for rental owners. No marketing is required. They already understand where the home is, how to get in, what the rules are, how to work things, and that the home meets their needs. **Repeat renters represent fewer headaches and more money.** These are happy renters, and you want to make sure that you keep them coming back. I like to offer discounts off new rates or a rate freeze at current rates to encourage repeat renters. As an owner, you will have frequent opportunities to make an offer to your current renters about the following year or possibly even subsequent visits during the current year.

Referrals

Using the golden goose analogy, renters referred to you by satisfied customers are the golden eggs! Referrals have a good opinion of your home already because of the recommendation from their friends and will largely know what they are getting. Some owners even offer a small discount (5-10%) to encourage referrals, payable either to the renter or the referral. Other than the possibility of offering discounts, there is no particular secret to generating referrals other than ensuring a quality vacation rental experience for your guests.

Retention of Client Contact Information

I referred earlier to the best kept secret in the property management business – that property

management companies consider renters of your home to be their customers and do not and will not share this information with owners. I was of course being a little tongue in cheek since there is no particular conspiracy afoot, it is just that most owners do not think about having client contact information until they decide to move their business to another firm or to self manage. At that point it is too late.

In all fairness, you can't blame property managers for this since they did do the marketing to bring these people in. Yes, I know, you paid the commission to support all of the marketing activity but that's just the way it works. And if you think of something clever to do about it (like I did), you will probably learn (like I also did) that it won't work. Here is my example of what I tried.

They're Just Business Cards for Goodness Sake!

I thought of creating and putting into the rental home a small, discreet stack of business cards with my name, address and phone number in case the renters wanted to contact me directly. How clever, huh! Upon one of my first visits to the home after dropping off my cards I discovered them missing. When I inquired with my customer service representative about this, she referred me to the company president, a good friend of mine. I sat down with him and after a few moments understood that he (and likely all firms) did not permit this direct contact and did everything possible to discourage it. No more business cards.

> **The only effective way for an owner to establish an ongoing relationship with their renters is to self-manage their rental home.**

Of course, you can wait and find this out the hard way like I did after you change property management firms. I encourage owner managers to keep good records of past visitors, particularly email addresses and telephone numbers, to permit direct and timely marketing under any circumstances. This information is a valuable asset which permits you to communicate with your renters from year to year, offer return discounts as desired and build you stable of return renters.

Tax Advantages

We will take a more thorough look at opportunities for tax savings on vacation rental property in later chapters, but I will mention one key tax advantage for owners in performing rental self management. From a tax point of view, it is generally more advantageous to be classified as a business owner than an investor. Two key criteria for making this distinction are 1) a requirement for owner involvement in management and 2) a demonstrated intent to make a profit.

> *TAX SAVINGS ALERT! An owner who assumes the responsibilities of their own rental management both increases owner involvement and demonstrates a clear interest in making a profit, two key business owner attributes for tax purposes.*

Home Maintenance and Condition

I think that I mentioned in the introduction to this book that owners who were particular about the condition of their homes were doubly well suited for self management. These are the owners who are most likely to be dissatisfied with the results achieved by using property management companies in terms of the monitoring and upkeep of their home. Decisions that are necessarily made without owner knowledge or input – after all, that's what you are paying them for – are sometimes not the same decisions that you would have made.

In addition, it is a common misconception that short term vacation rentals exact a higher price on the condition of the home than long term rentals – exactly the opposite is true! Frequent cleanings and visits by service personnel disclose potential problems before they get out of hand. Through self management, owners who want to keep their homes in excellent condition will likely benefit from having closer relationships with their rental clients, with cleaning personnel, with occasional service providers and with their maintenance contacts.

> *Owner/managers can expect their home to be maintained much more in keeping with their expectations simply because of more direct and frequent communication and feedback.*

Owner Control and Satisfaction

This is the BIG intangible and frankly one that means different things to different owners. I enjoyed tremendously the increased control that self management brought me in several areas: more control over income, more control over expenses, more control over renter relationships, more control over usage, more control in every way.

And my satisfaction increased also. I really enjoyed my rental business. I found it to be less stressful than dealing with a "go-between" at the property management company. I liked fixing up my home, anticipating what my visitors would like and how to improve their vacation rental experience. And I liked and benefited from the condition that my home was in when I stayed there. I had everything that I needed, I was happy with the condition of my home and I was able to take advantage of the times that my home was available to me since I was the scheduler. There is no question that I was more satisfied than ever with my rental homes after I took over rental management.

Chapter 3

Getting Started with Rental Self Management

I want to begin the journey to more income and control by addressing the principal requirements for rental home owner self management and get you focused right away on a few decisions that you will want to make in the very beginning. It will certainly be easier, less frustrating and more financially rewarding for you if I can help you to get your rental management program up and running quickly.

In this chapter, we cover what is required of the owner (that's you!) for rental self management and what kind of special issues exist for your rental home. We also consider critical policy decisions and some early action plans to undertake in preparing to rent your vacation home. An understanding of what is required will help you successfully begin your rental self management program.

- **What is Required of You?**
- **What is Required for Your Home?**
- **Critical Policy Decisions**
- **Early Action Plans**

What is Required of You?

The first thing that I recommend is to take stock of what you can and will bring to this effort. Self management is not for everybody of course. Some people prefer to not be involved with renting their own property for a variety of reasons. I have broken the basic requirements down into a few specific areas that you should focus on in order to assure your rental program success:

◊ **Time, Effort and Initiative**

◊ **Good Customer Service**

◊ **Quality Attitude**

◊ **Honesty and Candor**

◊ **Basic Computer Literacy**

Time, Effort and Initiative

One reason that you can expect to get benefits from rental self management is that you will be doing some of the work yourself. But, while it does take a little time, with the flexibility of email this can be accomplished on your schedule. Even if you are a fulltime employee, you can certainly manage your property yourself. *On the other hand, if you feel that you do not have a single minute to spare, you might not be a good candidate for self management.*

> *TAX SAVINGS ALERT! Your time and effort constitutes "active participation" in renting, one requirement to enable you to deduct some or all of your passive losses from renting your home.*

Your interest and initiative are the first requirements of being a successful rental manager. For me, it was clear that I wanted to be involved with my home and enjoyed doing so. I tend to like to take care of what I have and I am certainly downright enthusiastic about making more money!

Good Customer Service

As the principle, perhaps the only, point of contact with your renters, your personality and attitude will be very important to your success. You are the business and your renters are your customers. If you can't wait for the opportunity to work with people who are looking forward to a vacation, you are probably the right person for the job!

So much of the reward from both a personal and financial point of view relates to your enjoyment of working with your renters throughout the rental management process. What short term vacation renters overwhelmingly want is a happy, worry-free, memorable vacation. The more that you're able to let that happen, the more successful you will be.

Honesty and Candor!

In addition to realistic pricing, be certain that your property descriptions describe your home condition honestly in order to set realistic expectations with your renters. When potential renters call or email with questions, be accurate with your answers – the things that they inquire about are the things that they care about at that moment and all renters will not necessarily be looking for a place like yours. You can bet that any disappointment will result in more frequent "trouble" calls and/or complaints and fewer return renters.

At the same time, I do believe in "selling" my rental home – if I am not proud of my home, I surely can't expect the guests to be excited! Constantly try to increase your understanding of what the market is looking far. If there is something that can be improved easily or inexpensively to attract more occupancy, you should consider it.

Basic Computer Literacy

I am going to provide some guidance in a later chapter on what is required to electronically communicate and administer a program of self management. I am convinced that a principle reason that many people do not list their rental homes on the internet is simply fear based on a lack of knowledge of computers. However, it is in fact those very people who have the most to gain by increasing their exposure to the possibilities of the new economy.

> *Generally speaking, any owner who uses their computer casually on a regular basis probably has sufficient skills and knowledge to administer a program of rental self management.*

I recommend that even experienced users study the pages on computer basics to make certain that indeed you are covering all the bases – I assume that one reason you bought my book was to avoid the mistakes that I made!

What is Required for Your Home?

Throughout the course of this entire book we will be working toward the goal of assuring that your home is prepared to rent. In this chapter, we will review those things that are essential to a successful self management experience for your vacation rental home:

◊ **Desirable Property Location**

◊ **Home in Good Condition**

◊ **Reliable Guest Access**

◊ **Appropriately Furnished**

◊ **Primed and Ready to Go**

Desirable Property Location

Any short term rental program starts with having a desirable house in a desirable area. In order to charge rates and achieve occupancy necessary to justify the costs and efforts involved with a short-term vacation rental, the home must be sufficiently appealing for people to WANT to stay there on vacation. Earlier I referred to these issues of location and suitability for short term vacation rental as the "key rental factors".

Considering and looking for key rental factors before you buy a home is of course ideal, but if you already own your home you will include consideration of these factors as you determine rental rates, as you describe your home for marketing purposes and as you think about your target renter group. For instance, if your have a property targeted at beach goers, is the home located within walking distance to the shore? Renters will pay for the privilege of NOT having to drive and park in order to enjoy the ocean. If you have a mountain home, do you have the views that people visit the mountains to see? If you buy a cabin in a mountain hollow, it may be a wonderful place for you and your family to visit but it may not rent easily. Are you centrally located in your resort area so that you may appeal to families who are interested in varied options for different family members? If golfers are your target demographic, are there plenty of golf course choices nearby? I encourage rental home buyers and owners to be thoughtful and proactive in considering the location, size and suitability of their home as it relates to their target renter.

Home in Good Condition

After location, one real difference maker for achieving great internet rental success is the condition of the home. The fewest headaches occur with "A" properties for reasons that may be obvious. "A" properties are those that can be described with words such as "remodeled", "new appliances", "well kept", "extremely clean", First Class!" or the like. Property management companies often use scoring systems, but it is ultimately a judgment call and there is no better judge than you!

If you have a first class property in excellent condition, you have all options open. You may choose to self manage or elect to turn your home over to a property management company - they always welcome clean properties in good condition. If your home is less than an "A" property, particularly if it is in ragged shape and in need of maintenance and/or upgrade, you probably have what is termed a "C" or worse "D" property. If you choose not to bring the quality of your property up, you have only one choice – you should let a property management company handle your rentals.

> *Most owners will not want to deal with the headaches that come with self managing a property in poor condition.*

What would you do if you got a telephone call late in the afternoon on check in day and the customer complains about what they found when they arrived at your home? A property management company has other rental homes where they can move unhappy guests and you (presumably) don't. In addition, with a property in poor condition, the owner is also not likely to get the benefit of repeat renters and referrals.

Since all homes described in glowing terms will command higher rents, it usually makes sense to upgrade and otherwise improve your rental home. Keeping your home in top shape will also ensure fewer complaints and increase return rentals, a huge money maker as time goes by. And it is not always about spending lots of money but rather about attention to detail and taking care of obvious things.

The most important determinant of a renter's first impression is if your property strikes them as clean, bright and shiny when they walk in the door! Would you be any different? Start with paint. Remember, paint and caulk cover all sins! Then do a "deep clean" before your first renter and once every year thereafter. Deep cleaning must include blinds, window glass (inside and out), appliances (also inside and out) and floor moldings, some of the most frequently missed areas.

Reliable Guest Access

The biggest single physical problem that many owners face is providing for remote access to their home. Since a property management company is not involved in order to check guests in, the owner who self manages is obliged to establish a fool proof method of access.

Some owners have particularly difficult challenges with access, including condo owners who have to deal with building access in addition to access to their individual condo. The self managing owner ideally wants to avoid the use of keys altogether but, unfortunately, some homes, particularly condos, have common area restrictions that complicate the installation of lock boxes and key entry systems. I mention these issues now because you must have a workable access solution if you intend to do self-management.

Absent the above mentioned physical constraints, setting up remote (self service) access for the arriving rental guest is typically straightforward and will be covered in more depth in the "Rental Home Setup" chapter. I'll give you a hint: the answer is to use code entry systems which don't require the exchange of cards, keys or any other physical object.

Appropriately Furnished

By definition, short term vacation rentals are always fully furnished. Purchases of vacation rental homes often include furnishing, so you may be starting with someone else's idea of what should be in the home. Hopefully the previous owners considered durability, guest count and furniture function when they furnished the home. If you are furnishing a rental home from scratch, you will want to first read carefully the information in the chapter on setting up your rental home.

Primed and Ready to Go

Before any of your online rental sites go live, you must assure that the home is ready to receive renters.

Renters expect a turn key home when they walk in the front door. Cable TV on, temperature inviting, beds comfortable and clean and the home fully supplied.

Critical Policy Decisions

There are policy decisions to be made on a variety of issues that will affect everything from promotional text to the rates you charge. I suggest that you make these decisions early in the process by considering your choices in the following critical policy areas:

- **Do You Need to Consult an Attorney?**
- **Will You Accept Credit Cards?**
- **What about a Pet Policy?**
- **Do You Allow Smoking or Not?**
- **Will You Offer Accessibility for the Handicapped?**

Do You Need to Consult an Attorney?

Of course! I sometimes feel like I need legal advice just to get through the day! Seriously, I strongly recommend that you do not commit to an irreversible course of action with legal or tax implications until and unless you have spoken with an attorney or CPA depending on the nature of your inquiry. I tried to be my own attorney once and it almost cost me dearly, so I recommend seeking input from an attorney simply because it is often the best protection. For instance, this book cannot cover the range of state tax laws that, while generally following federal tax law, sometimes differ in significant ways. And while it is true that owners of single rental homes are often exempt from many of the state requirements to which professional managers are subject, you don't know what you don't know!

Specifically, you may benefit from having an attorney review your Guest License Agreement. Although the very existence of a contract often deters disputes, the more informed input you have, the better. Therefore, when you have prepared your preliminary *Guest License Agreement* as set forth in Chapter 10, consider that as the time to visit an attorney if you wish to. Admittedly, it can be difficult to find an attorney that knows the answers to landlord questions, but any attorney can do whatever research is necessary, and probably more effectively than you can.

Do As I Say, Not As I Do!

I have to be honest and say that I didn't take my own advice on this one. In my case, I started with a borrowed document and revised it thoroughly to suit me and my operating environment. I will say that I never had the least bit of trouble with my vacationing guests. My theory is that vacationers don't want any problems remotely associated with their vacation and, with all payments received in advance, I held all the cards. So I experienced zero contract disputes. But, remember; do as I say, not as I do!

Will You Accept Credit Cards?

If you want to be able to accept credit cards from renters, you will have to apply for Merchant Credit Card status in advance. **It is not necessary to have merchant credit card status in order to rent your seasonal vacation home, but it is the most practical way to handle 1) last minute reservations and 2) damage deposits.**

Although we will discuss payment issues later, I will say without equivocation that I had a perfectly acceptable experience being paid solely by personal check. **If you do not already have merchant status for accepting rental payments by credit card and you know that this is something that you wish to remedy, feel free to jump ahead to the Rent Payments and Collections section and consider applying now.** Keep in mind that providers generally DO NOT allow charges to be processed for different types of sales than those for which the merchant status was originally approved. If you want to move ahead without accepting credit card payments, you can always decide to apply later.

What about a Pet Policy?

You might as well go ahead and make a decision about allowing or not allowing pets into your home as it is definitely going to be important to both pet owners and non owners alike as they search for rental accommodations. You may have a personal bias on this subject depending on whether or not you own a pet and visit the home with your pet in tow. Indeed, you may have already made up your mind on this subject in which case feel free to skip the following discussion!

Reasons to Allow Pets - Before you struggle with this decision make certain that there are no local regulations or association rules preventing you from permitting pets in your rental home. A big positive is that allowing animals will likely result in more inquiries from potential guests looking for an option for taking their pet(s) on vacation with them. Pet owners who wish to bring their pets on vacation will not consider doing otherwise; they will simply continue to search for a rental that allows them to do as they wish. Since many hotels and other rental owners do not allow pets, your acceptance of pets could be a significant factor in your rental success. You may even be able to charge more by allowing pets, or charging more to guests who wish to bring pets and less to those who do not. There are many creative ways to approach this issue. With the correct safeguards, you can protect your property and financial interests, albeit with the distinct possibility of some extra effort.

Reasons <u>Not</u> to Allow Pets - There is almost certain to be more effort involved on your part if you decide to allow pets just because of the inherent issues with animals. Even if most pets are well mannered, there is always the risk that you will have the "bad apple" in your rental group! Also, keep in mind that a certain segment of the population is looking for rental housing that <u>specifically forbids</u> pets under any circumstances and your policy will garner their favorable attention.

My advice is to be realistic in approaching this subject whichever way you choose to go. And be prepared to stick with your decision since people who have pet allergies, etc. will notice and perhaps rightfully be disappointed if they find evidence of animals when they have been told that the home is "pet free". *After you make your decision on allowing pets, the most important issues concern how to publicize, encourage and enforce your policy.* Policy enforcement will be discussed further when we get to the section on leases in Customer Service and Communications.

Do You Allow Smoking or Not?

This is another fundamental policy decision that you should make and stick with. As with pet smells, non-smokers pick up on the smell of smoke like bloodhounds! In explaining your decision, avoid any hint of indignation or condemnation, but instead post your no smoking preference on the internet and describe your decision in a frank manner and as an economic decision. Further, I like to document somewhere in my household notices and in my rental contracts that burn marks are the responsibility of the renter. It is not likely that one would be successful in pursuing a financial remedy in the instance of minor damage, but this will help to encourage cooperation with your no smoking policy. As for signage, I recommend one polite reminder prominently posted somewhere in the home. If you permit smoking, provide plenty of ashtrays. If you do not, provide ashtrays anyway, along with guidance about smoking outdoors. And don't forget about the possibility of fire as a result of careless smoking habits – we will discuss fire prevention in Chapter 7.

Will You Offer Accessibility for the Handicapped?

You will need to decide early on if you are going to make the adjustments necessary to accommodate handicapped individuals. As a private individual renting your own home, you are not subject to the requirements of the Americans with Disabilities Act, assuming that you only have one rental property. However, accommodation of the handicapped can be a major opportunity to bring in additional rental inquiries. Think of how many families want to include an elderly family member in a vacation, and you get some idea of the extra appeal. If you have wide doors, or special bathroom features, or ground floor living and sleeping accommodations, you will want to make this point in your advertising and promotional material. If there are things that you can undertake to make your home more handicap accessible, you may want to start them now.

Early Action Plans

Although we will discuss some of these topics in more depth later, there are several areas where a few early decisions can rapidly get you moving toward your goal of owner management and increased rental income. After you consider each of these items, you will be in a position to decide what physical changes to make in order to prepare your home to receive guests. In this way you will avoid delay when you are otherwise ready to rent your home.

◊ **Providing Guest Access to the Home**
◊ **Creating Owner's Closets**
◊ **Undertaking Major Repairs**
◊ **Time Frame for Self-Management**

Providing Guest Access to the Home

Access is critical, and may require installation of locks. If you are not already committed to a particular course of action, read ahead to the section on Rental Home Setup to get guidance on this important topic. *After you have decided what your home access setup should be, order, install or otherwise arrange for exterior door locks and code/key access.*

Creating Owner's Closets

Consider which closets that you would like to hold back from guest use for owner storage. You must consider guest storage needs at the same time as you consider your own when deciding which areas in which to create closets. These decisions should be made early in order to allow time for physical modifications to be made. There is a full discussion of owner storage considerations in the Rental Home Setup section. *After you have decided on your owner closet setup, you should order, install or otherwise arrange for owner closet lockable doors and code/key access.*

Undertaking Major Repairs

Does your home require any repair? Be honest with yourself on this one. It's fine to postpone a repair or replacement to stretch your budget when you aren't renting, but you really don't want a failure of any kind if you can help it when you have paying guests in the home. After all, you should be generating some additional income, so consider it an investment.

There are certain types of failures you especially want to prevent like heating and cooling and hot water. State laws typically require that any landlord provide these essentials AT ALL TIMES, so you are required to make immediate repairs at <u>emergency rates if necessary</u> (!) if there is a renter in the home. If you don't mind ruining your ceilings by allowing a slow leak, though I don't recommend it, at least it is unlikely to impact your renter's current visit.

Keep in mind that the pace and outcome of repairs scheduled for open dates during the rental season is unpredictable and always includes the risk that you run into more than you anticipate. *Evaluate your rental home immediately, make a decision about which repairs need to be completed prior to guests arriving and get those repairs started.*

Time Frame for Self Management

Only you can decide when you and your home are ready for self-management. Your seasonal rental schedule will give you one possible target to shoot for if you are looking for some guidance: *you need to be ready at the very start of the reservation season.* You might be surprised to learn how early this can be. For instance, you should be online and ready to take reservations on January 1 for a spring and summer season because many people use the New Year as a trigger to get started, and they start fast on making reservations!

After you have read this book and have had a chance to decide what you need to do to prepare, come up with your own date to go live with your rental program. Whatever date you choose, it will arrive faster than you think, so get started!

Chapter 4

You Don't Have to be a Computer Expert

You don't have to be a "geek" by any means in order to successfully manage your own vacation rental home. When I started, I did have some background with Windows and knew how to use some fundamental applications like email and word processing. You're probably already familiar with basic computer functionality yourself, and I am talking "basic" here. I'm guessing that most owners who elect to self manage are at least mildly "internet friendly".

The fundamentals of email and hosting, word processing and browsing the internet are covered here, along with a brief discussion of digital photography - pictures are the key when it comes to advertising your home on the internet! After reflecting on this material, you should have a pretty good idea about what you need to learn, if anything, in order to handle the minor technical requirements of self management.

- **Email and Hosting**
- **Word Processing**
- **Internet Browsing**
- **Digital Photography**

Email and Hosting

Email will be your primary means of communicating with potential renters; in fact, it is probably not possible to take advantage of the opportunities for internet rentals if you don't use email. You will receive and answer inquiries from potential renters by way of email. You will exchange necessary documents with renters using email. You will keep track of your history of correspondence using email. Love it or hate it, email is part of the internet rental equation. It is important that owners of vacation homes who choose to self manage be comfortable with and frequently access their email. To some extent, your email options are related to whether or not you choose to create a dedicated website for your rental home in addition to listing it on the commercial web sites. We'll discuss websites in more detail in a later chapter.

◊ **Types of Email**
◊ **Hosting Your Email**
◊ **Controlling Junk Mail**

Types of Email

Aside from how you will connect to the internet which we will cover in the next chapter, the two big issues that you will make a decision about are 1) which of the two types of email software you will use and 2) who will host your email. Email is divided into two distinct categories: server-based and client-based.

Server-based

Server based email is just that; it resides on a server out there in internet land. When solely using server based email, your emails are never actually stored on your computer - you access your mail by accessing the server. Email providers such as Hotmail, Gmail, AOL, Road Runner, etc. are typically set up as server-based email solutions. An advantage of this approach is that your email history is available on the internet and can be accessed from anywhere that you establish connectivity. Disadvantages include the limited amount of data that you can store, lack of control over backup of email history and total dependence on the email provider's organization, presentation and functionality.

Client-based

Client based, or client server as it is often called, resides on your individual computer. Emails are downloaded and stored on your hard drive and thereafter may be accessed without connecting to the internet. You have access to your downloaded emails as long as you have access to your computer. The flexibility that you have for presentation and categorization of your emails is typically much greater, storage capacity is limited only by the physical size of your hard drive and you may construct your own "signature" information for outgoing emails. I use Microsoft's Outlook software to manage my emails.

> *I like the power and control over my email data inherent with downloading email into the client server software on my computer.*

Many users combine the best of both worlds. They frequently access their emails while the emails are residing on servers, but they also periodically download their emails onto their personal computer into a client server based program (such as Outlook) in order to control retention and allow access to previously downloaded emails when they are not online. With the proper settings for email retention and sharing, this dual approach offers the advantages of both server based and client based email in terms of flexibility, accessibility and control.

Hosting Your Email

There are three basic options for the domain name which you use for your email 1) free account providers, 2) at a hosted domain or 3) at your own domain.

- **Free Email Accounts**
- **Provider Hosting of Your Website**
- **Create and Host Your Own Domain**

Free Email Accounts

The aforementioned free email accounts such as Hotmail, Gmail, AOL, etc. are examples of free provider account solutions i.e. yourname@hotmail.com. Obviously, the free part is an advantage! The downside is that there are often constraints on commercial usage of these accounts. It is also true that your email addresses may lack a distinctive and professional sounding name. In addition, limited file sizes and message storage could be an issue depending on your particular usage. And finally, you want to make certain that the email address that you start your rental program with is the one that you are going to be using over the long haul – think repeat renters!

Provider Hosting of Your Website

If you elect to have a dedicated web site created for your rental home as many owners do, you may create one or more email addresses at that domain. Whomever you pay to host your domain will typically allow a number of email addresses, using your domain name, as part of the hosting cost. For instance, when we host web pages for clients at www.VacationHomeAdvisors.com, we include up to 5 email addresses for each of our clients at our domain using the client's rental home address i.e. yourname1@yourproperty.vhallc.com, yourname2@yourproperty.vhallc.com, etc.

The advantages of using an email address associated with your dedicated web page include that your email address is included with your hosting fee, your email address never changes as long as the hosting relationship remains in place and your email address always reflects your home address to remind recipients which property you own. More information on the options for a dedicated website is included in a later chapter.

> **Generally, the most practical solution for most owners is to outsource the creation and hosting of a dedicated rental home website to a specialty website provider.**

You may use the "signature" feature of your email to provide a link to your home's website. If you don't have a separate web site for your property, then the next best thing is to have your email signature refer directly to your individual property page on a commercial site on which your property is listed rather than to the commercial site homepage.

Create and Host Your Own Domain

If you are an accomplished programmer or wish to spend the money to pay someone else to do so, you of course have the option of creating your own custom web site for your rental home. If you want to purchase your own domain name and choose to pay to have it hosted, you may use email addresses associated with that domain name. For instance, if you own a hosted domain called *yourproperty.com*, you may choose to create an email address called yourname@yourproperty.com. An advantage of this approach is that your email address is owned and controlled by you as long as you own and host the domain – no more changing email addresses any time you need to change connectivity options or email hosts.

> *Independently creating, hosting and paying for a standalone website remains beyond the interest and abilities of most readers and, therefore, the scope of this book.*

Controlling Junk Mail

Whichever approach you take with your email, one common problem that you will always be dealing with is junk mail. Rather than go into a long dissertation on the subject. I will make only a couple of points. First, do not post your email address on the internet. Web crawling software is used by unscrupulous spammers to gather email addresses for use in sending junk mail. When we create dedicated web sites at www.VacationHomeAdvisors.com for our clients, we use an imbedded contact form to handle rental inquiries rather than posting your email address. Second, take the time and trouble to set up junk mail filters. These filters give you the opportunity to set tolerances so that you can control your own level of junk mail. The stronger the filter is set, the less junk mail is received but the more risk you take that you will unknowingly send a legitimate inquiry into your junk folder. Thus, it is important initially to review your junk mail folder to ensure that you have not missed emails that you would wish to receive. Over time, you will be able to make adjustments that minimize your unwanted email while assuring that good emails get through to your in box.

Word Processing

An important part of what you will do as your own rental manager is to create and manage documents of various kinds. Rental documents for your renters, marketing documents for the internet, informational documents for posting in your home, and other publications that you may choose to develop - the list goes on and on. Probably the most popular word processing software is Word, but Microsoft Works is included free on most PCs, and other brands of software should work just fine.

Skill Level

You don't have to be a great typist. Most people have some typing/keyboard skill in this day and age and I'm sure yours is sufficient – I've gotten by with the "hunt and peck" method for years. *The best friend of a poor typist is the knowledge of "copy and paste"*. Start by selecting existing text with your cursor or tool bar, and then select "copy". Move your cursor to the desired destination and select "paste".

Instant document creation! You will be pleasantly surprised how easily things can be copied from existing documents, from the internet, virtually from any source of text. You'll be an expert in no time!

PDF File Creator

Although you will create documents using a word processing program such as WORD, you will want and need to **save your WORD documents as PDF files before you send them** as attachments to your emails. A pdf file has several advantages:

◊ Pdf files are much smaller and therefore easier and quicker to both send on your part and to receive on the part of the recipient. This is especially important if one party is using a slow connection such as dial up.

◊ Pdf files appear as a printed page on your computer screen. No more worries about the document changing shape or size depending on what software it is opened in or what computer is used.

◊ Pdf files are not easily changed. This is important when sending leases, etc. to potential renters since you don't want to have to be constantly concerned that a subtle change has been made to the original of which you are not aware.

As you probably already know, Adobe Acrobat is available for free to everyone and is used to read .PDF files. Adobe makes their money by selling the software to *create* .PDF files at around $600 (pretty smart, huh?). However, an inexpensive option that I recommend for creating .PDF files is called pdffactory and is available at www.pdffactory.com for around $50. Other options abound.

Internet Browsing

Your Electronic Window to the World

The reason that self-management of vacation rental properties makes more sense now than 20 years ago is the access to your rental offering that the internet provides to literally millions of potential renters around the world. And just like these potential renters will use the internet to locate your rental home, *you may likewise find that internet access and exploration will enhance your rental ownership experience in many unexpected ways*. I use Internet Explorer for browsing the internet, but there are other browsing programs, some available free of charge.

Uses of Online Resources

This "window to the world" can contribute to your rental success by:

◊ Providing access to commercial rental marketing sites to enable you to market your home. Websites such as

www.Alexa.com rank commercial home rental websites in terms of popularity which can help you in choosing where to spend your marketing money.

◊ Allowing downloading of information that you can share with your guests. There is no quicker or more comprehensive way to do advance research on area activities, restaurant information, entertainment venues, etc. than searching the internet.

◊ Permitting evaluation of competing properties in your area to see what they offer, how much they charge, where they are located, etc. It just makes sense to check out the competition locally. You might even decide to "borrow" descriptive phrases or creative approaches that you find – it is not necessary to start from scratch on everything!

◊ Locating and contacting service providers to help in your rental and home management efforts. Along with the local telephone book and word of mouth referrals, searches of local service providers on the internet offers another method of checking out your options.

◊ Creating and providing maps and directions for your guests for their guidance and convenience. You may choose to print pdf maps, to imbed links to online maps in your email correspondence or to generate specific directions to your home, all for the convenience of your guests.

◊ Shopping for and purchasing supplies that you'll need for your rental home. Some specialty items for rental homes are easiest to locate using the internet.

I have provided a listing and discussion of a small sampling of online resources in Chapter 14.

Managing Your Internet Browsing Experience

There are numerous benefits provided by the internet, but you have to make some effort to increase your abilities and knowledge. If you have not otherwise done so, I suggest the following as a starting point:

◊ Become familiar with the browsing software of your choice, including built in tools for sorting and storing information.

◊ Become expert at "searching" the internet using one of the many "search engines" available such as Google, Yahoo, etc. These search engines are some of the most powerful information retrieval tools ever invented and you will find that they are of immense value in locating resources to enhance your guests' rental experience.

◊ Organize your online activities, including your "favorites" folders, to guide you to sites that you repeatedly find useful. It is not surprising that useful websites are visited time and again.

◊ Organize the results of your internet browsing into files and folders on your hard drive so that they may be easily found when you need them. I strongly encourage all users, but particularly business users, to save email attachments in separate folders on their hard drives and not to rely simply on client email programs for document retention and access.

◊ Access newsletters and organizations to support your rental efforts. Your electronic trips of discovery will uncover a wide range of supportive tools, information resources and related organizations which you will find helpful in managing your rental home.

> ***Provide helpful links and web addresses to your guests with your introductory letter in advance of their visit so that they may avail themselves of the information they need to plan their visit.***

It sends a very powerful message of good customer service when you go to the trouble to anticipate guest needs and provide them with resources which they may themselves use to heighten their vacation experience.

Digital Photography

Pictures are the secret to marketing your home!

No amount of flowery description will have as much impact as beautiful pictures. Take lots of pictures and use them regularly and in many different ways to assist you in your rental program. You will need pictures to upload to the commercial websites which you select, you'll need pictures for your own dedicated website, you'll need pictures to send in response to renter inquiries, even to show off to friends and relatives.

All So Easy and Inexpensive

Rather than paying someone else, learn to do your own digital photography. You will not only save money but will also give yourself flexibility in creating and updating your favorite images of your home. And it is all so easy and inexpensive with a digital camera. If you haven't tried it before or think that you aren't a good photographer, buy a cheap digital camera. Most digital cameras come with some basic photo software, and you can always upgrade to a more sophisticated product such as Photo Shop anytime that you wish to. Once you get the bug, you'll become proficient quickly.

Digital Photography Hints

◊ Keep your camera handy anytime you visit.

◊ You can't take too many pictures. Electronic images can be stored indefinitely at no cost. When you are ready to use them, they are there waiting for you!

◊ You'll want to make certain that any planned decorating is done before you take your website pictures. It doesn't hurt to photograph your unfinished living room with the old console TV, but it is probably better not to go to the trouble to post your pictures online until you have the finished product.

◊ You can't take too many pictures.

◊ Omit people from your photographs to encourage your customer to envision themselves in the picture!

◊ You can't take too many pictures.

◊ When you use your camera, be aware of a couple of minor technical issues, primarily lighting and framing, to make certain that your pictures turn out great. One of the great things about digital photography is that you can make mistakes inexpensively since you don't have to print out anything that you are not satisfied with.

What to Photograph

◊ Make certain that you get a picture of every room so that you can showcase them all in your marketing. Besides, you will eventually get a request or inquiry about a specific room or feature that is best answered by a photograph.

◊ Include pictures of the exterior under different lighting and weather conditions to make certain that you can showcase the best features of your home under a variety of conditions.

◊ Make certain that you capture all the special features of your home such as hot tubs, pools, decks, porches, swings, etc.

◊ Take photos of features that you are going to mention in your marketing, such as pools and decks, bedding arrangements, new furniture, or fancy kitchen appliances.

◊ Make sure to photograph the views available from different windows if they are appealing. Potential renters can imagine themselves enjoying the view!

◊ Try taking photographs from different angles and locations throughout you home and property. Sometimes a great shot is a matter of perspective!

◊ Take pictures of not only your home, but of your neighborhood, strong community features such as pools and playgrounds, area attractions like ski slopes, beaches, golf courses, etc.

◊ Take pictures in different seasons, especially if your rental home is available different times of the year. If your home offers something special for each season, you'll want to show it.

Chapter 5

Basic Hardware and Setup

The computer setup that you have at home today is probably perfectly sufficient to run your vacation rental program – a computer, a printer and an internet connection are the essentials. When you begin your rental program, you will be more dependent than ever on your computer for communication and record keeping. Hardware requirements are covered in this chapter, as well as your options for internet connectivity, how to ensure computer privacy and protection, and a few computer "housekeeping" chores. This is basic stuff, but preparation and planning is surely one reason you bought this book! Review of the following section will help you to ensure that your system is properly setup to manage the communication and computer requirements for a program of rental self management.

- **Computer, Printer and Phone**
- **Connecting to the Internet**
- **Information Privacy and Protection**
- **Computer Housekeeping**

Computer, Printer and Phone

Minimum Hardware Requirements

In addition to some modest knowledge, rental self-management will require a minimum amount of electronic hardware to efficiently work with renters. Could it be dome totally manually, without using a computer and email? The short, unequivocal answer is no, not really. Self management of rental properties is a function of the internet and the marketing and communication advantages that approach offers. If you haven't already made the leap, you will have to make a small investment in equipment. Our discussion will cover the following:

◊ **Telephone**
◊ **Computer**
◊ **Printer**
◊ **Scanning and Faxing (Optional)**

Telephone

Can you operate a rental program from your home using only your home telephone? I would say yes, as long as you have an answering machine and don't travel frequently or for long periods. You limiting factor is the need to be in touch in case of emergencies. We will discuss backup plans for your guests in case of power outages, lockouts, appliance trouble, etc. but, regardless of how well you prepare, you still should expect to be the contact of last resort. *It is for this reason that I rely on a cell phone as the principle point of contact with my guests*.

Computer

A laptop offers total flexibility in handling your rental affairs when you are away from home. You can access all downloaded emails and stored files from practically anywhere. *A desktop works just fine except when you are on the move*. If you are satisfied with using someone else's computer to check in or work while you are away from home, you may be able to get by with a "Flash" or "Thumb" drive. These are small solid state drives about the size of a stick of gum and are cheap. A Flash drive is a very convenient way for you to carry all your rental files wherever you go so that they are handy for communicating with renters from remote computers.

Printer

There will be instances where you will want to print out hard copy documents and a reliable printer can be had for under $100. While most renter communication will be by email, you will sometimes need to print out guest information, home postings, renter instructions, etc. More about guest communications later.

Scanning and Faxing is Optional

To really upgrade your office functionality, you might also consider your scanning and faxing capability. *I have always used a multifunction printer which offers scan and fax functionality in addition to basic printing.* This will eventually enable you to scan and store much of your paperwork and records on your computer, saving storage space and, even more importantly, permitting ready access to old records and documents. As this implies, you don't have to have a separate device anymore for sending and receiving faxes - with the right software, you can let your laptop do the job.

Connecting to the Internet

Accessing the Internet

Internet access is the basic foundation for your self managed rental business. Your property will be posted on the internet, you will find numerous essential resources at your disposal, and inquiries will come via email. We will cover the use of commercial rental websites in Chapter 11 and have a starting list of key web sites for rental home owners in Chapter 14. The need to access the internet varies with the individual lifestyle and preferences of the owner manager, but it will be at least occasionally. I suspect that most owner managers are well beyond occasional in terms of their interest and use of the internet.

Email is Critical

Let's focus on email connectivity since email will be the principle way that you communicate and exchange documents with renters and potential renters. Reliable email access is critical to your success. If your service is down for days at a time in the prime reservation season, you potentially could lose thousands of dollars of income. It is a best practice to ensure that you are able to access your email almost anytime and anyplace.

There are more options than ever for connecting to the internet and enabling email:

◊ **Public Access**
◊ **Dial-up**
◊ **DSL**
◊ **Coax and Fiber Optic Cable**
◊ **Cell Phone Service**

Public Access

You can go into virtually any library or coffee shop and many other locations throughout the world to access the internet. Some locations offer only connections, while others provide public access computers and working facilities, sometimes free, sometimes not. If you have a wireless receiver built into a laptop computer, you may take advantage of facilities that offer connections only. Of course, you can expect to pay for these services in most instances. I have found the inexpensive internet subscriptions offered by national chains like bookstores to be a reliable and convenient alternative. *I do not recommend relying strictly on free publicly available access to manage your rental business.*

Dial Up

Typically the slowest speed and therefore the most limiting for transferring large files, dial up remains a viable and usually less expensive option for those who have a land line telephone. If you go with this option, pick a service that offers toll free telephone numbers in the areas that you visit in addition to your local area. *A dial up connection works quite well as a low cost solution for managing a vacation rental from a fixed location.* As you probably already know, dial up service costs about $19.95 per month from an Internet Service Provider (ISP).

DSL

This service, offered by local telephone companies, is faster than dial up but not as fast as cable and slightly higher in cost than dial up. The connection is provided through your telephone line and coexists with your regular telephone service. *This service works best with a stationary computer, although generally emails may be accessed online when you are away from home if you have access to an internet computer.* However, your data files are not accessible remotely, only your emails. I realize that even this hurdle can be overcome with technology, but that discussion is beyond the scope of this book

Coax and Fiber Optic Cable

This is the fastest connection available. This option relies on cable, in many homes the same hard line as your cable television, which can carry large amounts of data very quickly. *This is the connection of choice if you work principally from a fixed location or have a home or work network with several users.* Like DSL, emails may be accessed online when you are away from home if you have access to an internet connected computer, but not your data files.

Cell Phone Service

It is certainly possible to manage your rental business through a cell phone connection. Emails are easily transmitted by cellular signal and the capabilities of "intelligent devices" such as the Blackberry and the iPhone offer enhanced performance and "app" capabilities. Cellular data service results in an additional monthly charge from your cell phone company but offers enormous advantages in flexibility and remote access. Cellular service may also be accessed directly through your laptop via a special modem card or by using a data ready cell phone as a modem. Emails are downloaded as they normally are, and you have access to all of the rental files necessary to proceed with the transaction. Using your cell phone to conduct your business is an impressive and efficient way to keep up with rental inquiries regardless of your personal travel schedule.

> *By combining cellular service with a laptop computer, you can conduct all of your rental business from virtually anywhere.*

I have used this technology for some time now. One of my favorite stories is how I took reservations and completed a transaction with a renter while I was happily ensconced in Yellowstone Lodge!

Information Privacy and Protection

Commit to the Basics

You don't have to be an expert to understand the basics of maintaining your computer to an acceptable level of security. On the other hand, even if you don't run a business or perform other critical tasks with your computer, you invite disaster if you don't employ some basic tools and tasks to protect your system. Addressing the following objectives is essential to achieving an acceptable level of protection and privacy for your computer:

- **Keep out Hackers and Viruses**
- **Eliminate Pop-up Ads and Spy Ware**
- **Reduce Unwanted Email**
- **Backup of Files and Settings**

Keep out Hackers and Viruses

I cannot emphasize enough that if you access the internet *you must have both anti-virus software and firewall software installed and running on your computer.* It is best not to have more than one security product active at one time for a given application. In addition to security programs that come with your computer operating system there are many well known purchased security and privacy software products such as McAfee, Norton, etc. Another alternative is to choose among the wide variety of free products available for download. All you have to do is Google free security software to come up with a broad selection. I have provided a couple of examples with which I am familiar in the chapter covering online resources.

Eliminate Pop-up Ads and Spy Ware

Although less important from a safety/security standpoint than the previously mentioned software, you might want to consider installing other free programs which will help you to keep your computer free of unwanted spy-ware, usage ware and popup ads. If you do not already use a commercial product like McAfee, Norton, etc. there are lots of free products available for internet download. You will find a couple of suggestions in the online resources chapter.

Reduce Unwanted Email

Keep in mind that when you hit "reply" or "reply to all" in an email, you are confirming the validity of your email address to the sender. You may occasionally receive bogus inquiries (or other solicitations) which you should ignore. Some are easy to spot: inquiries from other countries, inquiries with no detail, etc. But spammers can be so clever! How about when you receive an email that appears to be from your bank or other financial institution? A rule of thumb is to never click on a link in an email – if you believe that a legitimate inquiry has come in, contact the supposed sender directly by addressing your own email or making a telephone call. Use common sense in deciding which inquiries are legitimate and which are not and always be a little suspicious.

Spam blocking software can be used to block out unwanted and unsolicited email, and is frequently included with purchased security or utility software or can be accessed on your email provider's server. However, anti-spam software may cause at least some rental inquiries to be blocked. In order for it to perform properly, you must carefully review all of the email messages that either your standalone spam blocker or your mail server rejects for the first 90 days. If you learn how to revise the built-in rules so that important email is not accidentally deleted, then it might work for you. *If you're doing business on the Internet, I recommend that you go ahead and manually review all of your own incoming email.* Receiving and responding to all rental inquiries is too important to your rental program success to take a chance that an incoming email may be accidentally overlooked.

Backup of Files and Settings

Short Term Data File Backup

AVOID DISASTER by backing up all important data files on your computer (not including programs) in case your computer hard drive is damaged or your data is otherwise lost. Although the operating system, all applications and your program settings can be reloaded in the event of a software or hardware failure of your system, your <u>data files</u> will be lost if not regularly copied to a storage medium independent of your internal hard drive. The Flash drive mentioned in the previous section addressing required resources is a very easy and recommended way to backup – you just plug it in to you computer, copy the correct folder containing your real estate and other critical files onto it, and you are good to go! Plus, it can be reused over and over again. The only caution is to not loose your flash drive – they are so small. I like to attach a strap or key chain to help keep track of mine. *I recommend doing a short term backup every day or two, depending on how many days of work that you think that you can afford to lose!*

Long Term Data File Backup

REGULARLY backup your entire hard drive or at least the folders that are used for storing business related files. Since you are storing larger amounts of data, you will might need a large capacity external drive. Even a hard drive backup should take only minutes and you invite disaster if you do not take the time to do it.

Files and Settings Transfer

A more extensive backup process will result in certain settings being saved as well as data files. This involves using the Windows accessories utility called Files and Settings Transfer Wizard, found in Windows XP at Start/Programs/Accessories/SystemTools. By selecting and storing separately all your files and application program settings, you are prepared to reload them onto your new or reconfigured computer should you have a major problem such as a drive meltdown. Caution: Take care to select the .pst file extensions in addition to the standard files if you use Outlook Client Email. The Transfer Wizard default settings will not back up your emails and contacts otherwise, an important issue for those conducting business electronically.

I recommend backing up __all__ your files at least every two to four weeks. This will guarantee that you do not accidentally lose a file change that you neglect to capture in your short term backup routine.

Off Site Storage

Finally, keep in mind that it is a good idea to occasionally store critical data offsite in the event of a true catastrophe. In this manner, even the worst of circumstances and bad luck won't force you to start from scratch – you can go back to the old version and start from there! Obviously, like with any backup process, the more often that it is done, the less work is lost in the event of a failure. Major companies have been doing this for years and, even if you do this only sporadically, at least you will have something to work with if the totally unanticipated occurs. Think Hurricane Katrina!

Computer "Housekeeping"

Keeping Your Computer in Good Working Order is Important

This may be the most technical section of the whole book so if you are comfortable with how your computer functions, you may skip it. It is only related to rental home management in the sense that you do rely on your computer for communication and record keeping. Therefore, it is critical that you ensure uninterrupted service.

There are a few things that every computer user needs to know to keep things running smoothly, even if they don't do business over the internet. Have you noticed your computer reacting sluggishly or freezing up periodically? That is a sure sign that you need to perform some system maintenance. You may certainly take your computer to a technician if you wish, but the good news is that you don't need to pay someone else to do basic maintenance for you. *I guarantee that if you improve your computer's performance, you will improve your entire computing experience.* Even if you just use your computer to play Tetra, you will want to practice several maintenance and good housekeeping tasks including:

- **Empty the Recycle Bin**
- **Organize Data into Folders**
- **Clean Your Hard Drive**
- **Defrag Your Hard Drive**
- **Clean Your Registry**

Empty the Recycle Bin

I occasionally delete files unknowingly that I later wish I had saved. Thanks to the Windows functionality of automatically transferring files which are "deleted" to the Recycle Bin folder located on the Desktop, retrieval is usually possible. However, if the Recycle Bin is crowded with files, finding your good file among the many that you do not wish to restore can be difficult, especially if you are not certain of the name of the missing file. For this reason, I like to empty the Recycle Bin frequently.

Organize Data into Folders

You know how much easier it is to find something in your closet when you have taken the time to put things in order beforehand? Or what about locating your car title when you have had the foresight to create a special file in your desk drawer for "Automobile"? The requirements for efficiency and order in your electronic life are much the same. *You should spend some time on a regular basis creating folders of your own description in which to organize files and references on your computer.*

Clean Your Hard Drive

Often when you access the internet, install new programs or perform other routine activities, your computer stores extra miscellaneous files on your hard drive. *Removing these extra files is akin to taking out the trash – if you don't do it periodically, it may not shut down all household activities, but things could start to smell!* The solution is simple: go to C:Start/Programs/Assessories/System Tools/Disk Cleanup and run the program.

Defrag Your Hard Drive

It may surprise you to know that your computer stores individual files in numerous pieces all over your hard drive and links the pieces by an index! This is to ensure that all the space on your hard drive is available for storage. Over time, unfortunately, this "inconvenient convention" has to be corrected or performance will suffer dramatically. Imagine how much your disk drive will have to spin to reassemble all these little 'Humpty Dumpties" as they become increasingly fragmented.

"Defragging" your hard drive will provide extraordinary improvement if it hasn't been done lately (or ever!). If you are a windows user, go to C:Start/Programs/Assessories/System Tools/Defrag to find both the cleaning and defrag tools. Use of this tool is self-instructional and can be extremely beneficial for your computer's performance. Be aware, however, that the defrag process may take hours depending on how much file reassembly is required. This is a perfect activity to get your system started on when you retire for the night.

Clean Your Registry

If you have kept up with the "user friendly" security and maintenance items discussed above and still have problems, don't be ashamed to take your computer to the shop for repair and ignore the following paragraph. However, cleaning the registry on our computer only requires purchase and use of a utility program and a desire to understand more technical aspects of the computer. The registry is the set of instructions that are executed by your computer every time that you start it up. As you use your computer, different instructions and bits of code are added to your registry to change what happens upon startup. Although cleaning your registry is not required on a regular basis, your registry will over time become compromised by normal activity and other changes, eventually resulting in poor computer performance.

Keep in mind that, in addition to cleaning your registry, a complete utility program optimizes the performance of your computer, solves problems and helps you to customize your system. In this respect, it lets you make your system faster, easier to use and more secure in a matter of minutes. A complete utility software package should combine system optimization, configuration, cleanup and maintenance in a modern graphical user interface. Or you can just buy a good registry cleaner! The one that I use is Registry Mechanic which is available for around $30.

Chapter 6

Prearranged Home Services

Partnering with reliable service providers is as important as any responsibility you will undertake in managing your vacation rental home. Even if you live near your rental home, you will depend on your service partners to perform what they have committed to do when they commit to do it. The further that you live from your rental property, the more you will depend on your cleaning and maintenance contacts to inform you about conditions with your home. Organizing an effective cleaning regimen and preparing in advance for ongoing maintenance and for major repairs is critical to your rental management success. This chapter will help you to know what to look for when arranging housekeeping service or when establishing partnering relationships. Preparing in advance will help you to avoid or address the household problems and surprise expenses (not to mention aggravation) which always seem to arise at the most inopportune times!

- **Housekeeping**
- **Maintenance**
- **Repairs**

Housekeeping

There is nothing more important to the renter than to feel that they are staying in a clean home. Some people are absolutely obsessive about it. In most self management situations, the success that you have with housekeeping will determine how good you feel about the entire rental self management process. We are going to discuss several issues that are central to gaining control of and confidence with your cleaning regimen.

Housekeeper Requirements

Hiring your housekeeper or cleaning service will be a very important decision, and you may not get it right the first time. Even if you do get it right, circumstances change so keeping a close eye on your housekeeping will always be important. Understanding the key performance criteria for this job is a good place to start.

Reliability: You must be able to depend on your housekeeper to show up as arranged and to do what is required. This is the single biggest issue. Housekeeping for a rental home is obviously very different than when you hire someone to clean your own home. With a rental property, there is very little room for error when it comes to showing up and doing the job.

Time Sensitivity: You home must be cleaned on time, every time and the job must be complete before your posted check in time. I established a check out time of 11:00 AM for departing guests and a check in time of 4:00 PM for arriving guests to allow time for a cleaning if I had back to back rentals. Of course, if renters arrive early, that is not the responsibility of the housekeeper, but this is another area where a little flexibility goes a long way. At the very least, I always allowed guests to drop off luggage if they got in town early, and tried to allow them in the home as soon as the cleaning was done.

Quality: Only some experience, renter feedback and maybe a few owner inspections will show if the cleaning is done completely and satisfactorily.

Backup Plan: When you require rapid turnover for back-to-back rentals you can't afford to hire an individual who doesn't have a plan to cover your home in the event of their illness or incapacitation.

Owner Responsibilities

Coordinating housekeeping is an ongoing process that can't be taken for granted, so understanding the requirements and challenges is important.

Hire a Good Housekeeper: Check with other owners in your area to find out who they use. Personal recommendations are the surest way to start off right.

Liability Coverage: Talk to your insurance agent about your rental home coverage. Make certain that you have landlord's insurance and verify that housekeepers are covered.

Respect and Dignity: Treat all service personnel with respect. You will receive better performance and communication from a good relationship. Thankfully the Leona Helmsleys of the world are few and far between!

The Hiring Decision

Based on the feedback you receive from other owners in the area, you may be able to develop a short list of individuals and companies to consider. I suggest that you discuss the assignment with at least three providers before you select one. If you like the others ok, consider that you have contact information and groundwork already done if your first choice doesn't work out. Depending on who is available in your area, one important variable that you will decide on is whether to hire an individual or a company. There are advantages and disadvantages of both.

Hiring Individuals

Individuals who clean homes for rental owners are typically independent contractors so no withholding or payroll taxes are required on the part of the owner. After initial contact to verify interest, I suggest that you request an in-home interview with any potential housekeepers so that they may see the home first hand. When you set up the interview, ask them to bring a copy of their business license with them and any information on bonding or insurance that they have claimed. During the interview, there are several specifics that you will want to cover.

Cleaning Responsibilities: House cleaning is not rocket science but does involve dedication and effort and a clear understanding of responsibilities. The keys is to agree with your housekeeper on what needs to be done, and then for you to do some follow-up on occasion to verify good performance. If the job is consistently sub par, trust me when I say that you will hear about it from your renters. I am not going to try to describe what an acceptable cleaning job entails, because "cleaning checklists" are easy to come by. Rather than telling the housekeeper in detail what you expect, I suggest that you let them tell you what they include in their cleaning regimen based on their experience. You will get a pretty good feel about their knowledge of what is required to clean a rental home by listening to what they say.

Pay: Pay is usually negotiable, but bargaining someone down to rock bottom might not be in your best interest. We discuss the potential to save money on housekeeping in our chapter on lowering expenses. Nonetheless, pay your independent housekeeper fairly and you will likely still save plenty compared to professional cleaning firms who typically charge more in order to cover overhead.

Work Load: Ask about their work load to be certain that they are not over committing their time. How many other homes do they clean? Are they in your area? Are they rental properties with similar renter turnover? If they have five homes to clean and they are all weekly rentals with Saturday turnovers, you might anticipate some problem.

References: If the individual did not come to you by way of recommendation, ask for references. Before you make your final decision, contact the references that they provide and verify their good record.

Contact Information: I like to communicate with my housekeeper by email because I can communicate any time of day or night, because I can be precise in what I say and because there is a clear record of what was said and agreed to. Naturally you will want to record housekeeper phone numbers as well.

A Great Housekeeper Experience

As it turned out, once I moved to self management, I ended up hiring individuals instead of companies to clean both my mountain rental home and my beach property. I could not have made a better choice for my beach house. The lady that I hired was excellent, not only because she was conscientious but because she never missed an appointment. The only time she did not personally clean my home was when she was required to make an out of town trip. She let me know several weeks in advance and made sure that the cleaning was covered by family members. I had no complaints and to this day I still get good reports from one of my clients to whom I recommended her. All in all, this was a very successful experience. One final note: Don't judge a book by its cover. This lady preferred to clean barefooted! Turns out she thought that was a good test of whether the floors were clean. I think that she was right!

Hiring Companies

Neighbor recommendations may be for a cleaning company that they use instead of an individual. If you have trouble coming up with personal recommendations, then go to the phone book. Many of the same interview objectives apply as with individuals. Generally speaking, with cleaning companies, you can expect to pay more but you may be rewarded with less stress and more reliability. I say this because these companies employ multiple individuals and internal personnel problems are seldom apparent to the homeowner.

Watch for Warning Signs

Let me relate another personnel experience. I told you about my good experience with the housekeeper at my beach home; now I'll share an experience that did not work out quite as well. At my mountain home, I hired a woman who was obviously not overly sophisticated but certainly seemed to have the desire to do the work. Things started off fine for the first several months, but during the heart of the winter ski rental season I started noticing some problems, primarily with her missing scheduled cleanings. At first it was just a single missed cleaning which we managed to recover from, but things continued to deteriorate. The next sign of trouble was when she requested that I pay her a big advance lump sum payment for the coming month, which of course struck me as highly unusual. When I didn't come through on that, she disappeared entirely and I was left scrambling to cover my cleaning requirements through the thick of the rental season. I subsequently found out that she had become addicted to crack cocaine, which explained both her failure to show up and her request for a cash advance (not to mention her missing teeth but that's probably too much information).

Annual Deep Clean

At least once per year, typically right before your primary rental season, you should make arrangements with your housekeeper to perform what is called a "deep clean". This is a thorough cleaning of your home that goes far beyond the normal weekly cleaning that you expect on a regular basis. Things like washing windows both inside and out, wiping down moldings and trim, and scouring all appliances are included. Mattress covers, comforters and spreads must be dry cleaned or washed. In short, everything that isn't cleaned otherwise during the year will be covered in this day long effort. The cost is extra, but unless you as the owner are prepared to do it yourself, you are going to have to just pay up.

Cleaning Supplies for Guests

We have already touched on the question of cleaning closets and housekeeper supplies. But what about guests - should you leave cleaning supplies available for them? I always advise leaving a supply of safe cleaning products, garbage bags, carpet spot remover, mops, brooms, brushes and a vacuum cleaner in your seasonal rental home. You may find that guests sometimes clean up after themselves, making it easier for the cleaning crew. I found that providing a hand held, wall mounted vacuum made my guests happy and incidental cleanups easier. Put one on every floor if you really want to help the guests help you with upkeep. A word of caution: cleaning supplies can be a potential hazard and thus need to be left in a secured location. In addition, don't leave items that are particularly caustic, such as oven cleaner, available for even adult guests. In my opinion, it is just not worth the risk. For further information, see the section on Guest Safety.

Linens

"Linens" is the commonly used term (at least in the South) for sheets and towels and other textiles which are made from cotton or man mad materials, not linen. Although in some vacation rental markets it is still common practice to have renters bring their own sheets and towels, for the most part this practice is fading as renters tend to favor low maintenance solutions to reduce vacation stress. For most owners, the preferred solution is to furnish linens with the rental.

Purchase Considerations for Linens

I recommend that you purchase at least two complete sets of sheets, towels and washcloths to allow for turnover from one rental guest to the next. If you find a great source and decide to purchase a type, style or color that is unique, consider buying more than two sets to account for the damage, loss and destruction that inevitably occurs over time. I have heard some owners say that they like to provide color coordinated linens for their rental home for various good reasons that I don't argue with. However, I prefer to stick with white for the simple reason that they not only give the impression of cleanliness, they also can be washed in hot water and bleach to ensure that they are sanitary. A secondary advantage is that color coordinated replacements are easy to come by when the only color you have is white!

Bath Linens: Purchase towels, wash cloths and bath mats. I recommend that you purchase extra towels and cloths to account for shrinkage, especially the wash cloths. They often are used for unintended purposes and must frequently be replaced. Shop for comfortable and durable towels, but don't get them too large, especially if you live around water. Remember that they will be washed frequently and heavy towels can really tax the washer and dryer. For my home at the beach, I made it a point to include beach towels on my list of things for guests to bring.

Bed Linens: When shopping for sheets and pillowcases (what we in the South call "bedclothes") think more about comfort. This can be another one of those differentiating items for your home that you can and should tout in your promotional description. I only bought high quality products such as 300 thread count Egyptian cotton sheets. You may save a good bit of money on these high end linens if you shop at a store for "seconds" and "factory overruns". I realize that polyester in the blend extends the product life, but the reduction in comfort is substantial so be cautious.

Cleaning Options for Linens

There are three main options for cleaning your linens between guests:

◊ Your cleaning person may take them to his or her home to wash and dry and return them on the following trip. This reduces the in-home cleaning time and allows the housekeeper to take care of this chore at their leisure. The downside for the housekeeper is of course that it is their own washer and dryer that incur the heavy usage.

◊ If you have the in home capacity, your housekeeper may elect to do laundry while they are cleaning the home if time is available. This typically requires a high capacity washer and dryer depending on the size of the home, number of bedrooms and number of guests. The housekeeper starts work by putting in a load of laundry and, by the time they finish their other chores, the laundry is done.

◊ For very large vacation homes (more than 3 or 4 bedrooms), you may want to consider using a "linen service." In many vacation areas there are companies that will pick up dirty sheets and towels at the end of the rental period and replace them with fresh ones. You will still have to have your cleaning person make the beds and hang the towels in the bathrooms. If you are considering this option, be sure and determine if the service supplies the linens before you purchase them yourself.

Remember the Extras

You will need to provide blankets for all beds. This is especially important in cold climates since guest health, comfort and even safety depended on it (if you lost heat, for instance, during a cold snap). I also always used pillowcase liners which kept my pillows more sanitary and in generally better condition. This was another one of those differentiators because I could advertise that I had hypoallergenic pillows and liners.

Maintenance

Routine calls regarding non emergency maintenance received on a weekday generally will present no particular problem for the owner. There is time to check with a local service provider, negotiate costs, consider options carefully and schedule maintenance at a convenient time. Your major frustrations in managing your rental home are likely to involve those rare but inevitable calls you will receive on Friday evening around 5:00 PM that just can't wait: the hot water is out, the home heating or air conditioning has mysteriously stopped functioning, water has begun puddling in the kitchen, etc. Trust me on this one as I have experienced them all. It is uncanny how these things emerge right before the weekend begins, particularly right before long holiday weekends! *Your principal defense against pain and suffering, not to mention guest refunds and relocations, is going to be a prearranged network of service technicians and your own preparation.* With a roster of service people arranged in advance to contact, the rental homeowner can quickly and efficiently address any maintenance issues.

◊ **Recurring Maintenance**

◊ **Pest Control Contracts**

◊ **Maintenance Contracts**

◊ **Guest Feedback**

Recurring Maintenance

Battery Replacements

Battery replacements fall into the "most overlooked" category but are important to remember because batteries are in critical systems in your home. CO and smoke detectors usually are either exclusively battery operated or have battery backup, so battery changes are necessary to ensure correct operation. Just as critical are the batteries in your door lock and access system, which if neglected can definitely cause problems. Let me tell you how I got caught on this one.

This Could Have Been a Much Bigger Problem

One evening after visiting my beach rental house I was driving back to my primary residence and was about two hours away. My cell phone rang; it was my new arrivals and they couldn't get in. Seems the front door lock was not working and they couldn't get into the home! We verbally verified that they were using the correct code, but nothing worked. I called my trusty housekeeper who, fortunately, was still in the general area. She saved the day with a visit and, using her door key, let my guests in. The next day, I called maintenance and, as it turned out, the battery in the front door code lock had expired. I didn't even know that there was a battery in the front door lock! Besides changing the dead battery, I instituted a backup access system immediately.

Filter Changes

A filter is a low price item, and as such is the single most cost effective and important factor in assuring the low cost, continuous and efficient operation of several home systems. Your HVAC system is likely the most expensive system in your home. Air filters must be changed regularly depending on their type and the conditions in your area. I like to leave a box of the correct size and desired type in the home where they are accessible such as in the top of a closet. In this manner, the filters are convenient for the cleaning or maintenance people to change whenever necessary. Another key filter is on your dryer. Make sure that it is in good condition and encourage your housekeeper and guests to clean it after every use. The last filter that I will mention is the water filter that is usually found in modern refrigerators that have a through-the-door water dispenser. Although this filter only requires changing infrequently, be aware of it and arrange to have a replacement on hand.

Freeze Precautions

When sub freezing temperatures are forecast which might cause frozen pipes or freeze related problems, be certain that the unit heat is on (55 degrees minimum), open cabinet doors, and drip water in the faucets as a precaution. Tap water is warm enough to protect the pipes except in the most extreme cases. During periods of extended cold temperatures, have someone check for any evidence of frozen or burst pipes. If a frozen pipe situation occurs, shut off the water to the unit to prevent damage until repairs are completed. At the end of the low temperature period, return to the home and cut off the dripping faucets, close the cabinets and check the thermostat.

Extreme Weather Preparation

For beach property owners, it is important to have someone visit the home if a hurricane arrival is imminent in order to move all outdoor furniture to a secure location. Some homes have other built-in protections like window covers or storm shutters, but these generally require human intervention as well, so be prepared to deal with this personally or contact your maintenance company well before the last minute.

Nuisance Calls

These occur when guests are not familiar with a home (i.e. switches off, breakers tripped, lamps unplugged, etc.). In my opinion, it is preferable that the guest call me rather than struggle for a solution. If you get recurring nuisance calls on the same issue, that is a pretty good indication that you might want to fix the underlying source of confusion, or at least post detailed guest instructions.

Pest Control Contracts

My coastal and mountain homes were very different when it came to bugs and treatment costs. In the mountains, I only had to be concerned about flies getting in the home and the occasional spider and I did not incur any cost to speak of.

In coastal resort regions, you're going have bugs. Hire an exterminator and get on a program of regular spraying.

> **In tropical climates, remind your guests that if they see a lot of DEAD bugs, it means the exterminator is doing a good job!**

I also paid the upfront and yearly renewal costs of a termite deterrent system for around my home. If you choose to do so, make certain that you get a repair and replacement bond, not just a fixed payout.

Maintenance Contracts

Some rental homeowners, particularly those not living near their rental homes, choose to pay an annual fee to have a maintenance company function as a general contractor for maintenance. Maintenance company personnel respond directly to maintenance requests or coordinate and manage vendors and subcontractors as required. Paying for a single point of contact usually costs more but can lower time, effort and stress and is worth it to many owners. Annual contracts are typically payable in advance and provide modest discounts on hourly rates for repairs and a program of inspection and recurring maintenance depending on the company. A typical contract for maintenance may be organized as follows.

◊ **Beginning Walkthrough**

◊ **Annual General Inspection with Written Report**

◊ **Spring AC Inspection**

◊ **Fall Heating Inspection**

Be certain that you have a clear understanding with your maintenance company about who may authorize work to be done i.e. owner only, guests, housekeepers. Depending on your desired level of involvement, you may decide (like I did) that I wanted all repairs to go through me or you may decide to allow a trusted housekeeper to make the repair request independently. Remember to provide key and code access information to maintenance personnel in order to permit quick response to guest access issues if they arise. If you have service contracts for appliances, be sure to provide copies of the contracts to maintenance contractors to permit arranging of warranty service. Under all circumstances, agree on a "not-to-be-exceed" spending cap (say $200) above which owner approval is required (except in emergency).

Guest Feedback

Establish a way for guests to provide feedback on emerging or minor issues they experience so that you may address them before they become major problems. I tried several methods with varying degrees of success until I simply asked the guests to call or slip a note under the door of the owner's closet. I did get some good suggestions this way and it provides your guest with the satisfying sense that they can address minor annoyances.

Repairs

Any home is going to need repairs sooner or later whether it is a rental or not. As I have said before, although it may seem a little counterintuitive, short term rentals do not suffer from damage as frequently or severely as long term rentals. Even given the extra traffic, the short term rental home is more monitored and protected due to the regular visits from cleaning personnel, the short duration of stays and the security deposit! Nonetheless, you should expect that you will have to make repairs and improvements from time to time.

Establishing a Network of Contractors

Many second home owners don't live near their vacation home and therefore must rely on the help of others. Some multifamily properties have a local manager to maintain the grounds, remove trash or provide snowplowing. Other services must be arranged by you, such as for repairs and maintenance of the home. The good news is that there is often a large population of qualified vendors in resort areas from which to choose. The list of required support contractors will vary with the individual home and often includes plumbers, electricians, appliance technicians and other trades. When necessary, you may have to use specialty technicians for certain jobs such as carpet installation, exterior cleaning and painting, major carpentry, wallpaper hanging or removal, broken windows, screens or glass, exterior fence and deck repair, wall or ceiling damage, roof repair or replacement, etc.

Selecting Contractors

A proven way to locate good service providers is simply to initially ask your neighbors, then subsequently to rely on your own experience. All services for which you do not have a contract are negotiable. I recommend getting three bids before making up your mind on major projects. Once you are comfortable with a company or technician, checking prices may be limited to an occasional inquiry. Obtaining bids is time consuming for all concerned and, for small projects, not always necessary. Performance is ultimately what matters most to the absentee owner. Post instructions in your home for guests to follow in case of maintenance issues. For me, this always included my telephone number.

Chapter 7

Rental Home Setup

There are several straightforward but important considerations in physically preparing your home for seasonal rental. We will discuss setting up home access, review owner and guest storage, share ideas for your guests' safety, and consider a home inventory and setting up your rental home with needed household items. Once your home basics are in order, your renters will more likely experience a safe, sound and functional visit, and you will have increased protection for your home and for yourself!

- **Home Access and Security**
- **Guest Safety and Accident Prevention**
- **Addressing Storage Issues**
- **Home Inventory and Setup**

Home Access and Security

Earlier in this book, we touched on the importance of ensuring reliable home access for your guests. Consider all of your options as you read through this section, then make the necessary arrangements. Access is the physical cornerstone of your rentals. You have to come up with a workable solution that fits your circumstance.

Let's consider the critical components of a successful access plan.

- **Convenient and Reliable Access to Your Home**
- **Primary Home Access Plan**
- **Backup Home Access Plan**
- **Frequently Asked Questions about Access Locks**

Convenient and Reliable Access to Your Home

It is critical that arriving guests get into the home easily and seamlessly without owner involvement. The home must be locked and secure between rental visits, but easily and reliably accessible for renters and their families when they arrive. Some owners live in close proximity to their rental home and can manage the check-in personally, but many do not live locally and therefore have to be certain that they have foolproof plans arranged in advance.

While I have heard some "experts" talk about mailing keys here and there, this makes no sense to me whatsoever. A code accessible door lock, along with a backup system, is a far superior method and virtually foolproof. There are numerous variables that can effect your decision about the particular lock that you choose. Do you have a home with more than one entrance, or a condo in a high-rise? Are you in a dry inland setting, or located near the ocean? How much do you want to spend?

I have a friend with a condo in a building that restricts entry from the street by way of plastic electronic cards. This presents a challenge in that he must mail the access cards to the renter as part of the rental process.

I will state unequivocally that you must have reliable primary access and emergency backup access plans if you are going to self-manage your rental home.

Primary Home Access Plan

I swear by a keyless code system that has a key override. The override is not so much for renters since there will be a backup system for them. The override exists to enable cleaning or maintenance people to replace batteries or otherwise repair the system should it malfunction. A code access lock will permit your renters to enter a code into the door lock and gain access to the home.

For your primary access system, I advise that you not scrimp on cost. I strongly encourage you to invest in a sophisticated built-in code lock entrance system if possible. Your whole rental self management system will break down if the renter can't get into your home! Some of these locks are very attractive and functional, but can be a bit expensive at $275 to $500 per door for the lock. In addition, they require the assistance of a locksmith for installation, the cost of which may run from $75 to $150. Available in mechanical or electronic models, these locks come with a variety of features and options depending on your needs and resources. I consider the SIMPLEX 5000 Series (pictured next) to be a very good option and representative of this high end category.

The last time I checked, this lock was priced at $338 just to give you an idea. It and many others like it are available online, at your local hardware store or through a locksmith. In addition, there are some very good and less expensive locks comparable to the SIMPLEX brand, such as the CODELOCK brand, so feel free to do your own research. The features that I consider to be of most importance are 1) dependability and quality of the lock mechanism, 2) a key bypass feature and 3) the durability of the finish.

Backup Home Access Plan

It is also important to include a plan for backup access for your guests in case the primary access lock fails. The two principal backup options are to 1) have a redundant lock box located on the property or 2) make prior arrangements with a local trusted party to keep an override key in case of emergency. Better still, do both.

Using code activated lock boxes enables you to provide access over the phone in unusual circumstances without relying on the availability of your local contacts. One good, inexpensive arrangement, particularly suitable for a backup system, is one where keys to exterior doors are stored in real estate type lock boxes with mechanical code buttons and are hung from exterior door knobs or attached with screws to the home. An entrance key is then left in the box for guest use. These locks are also available at hardware stores and locksmiths as well as online. Expect to spend from $35 to $50 dollars per box. In addition to the advantage of low price, they don't require professional installation.

The primary disadvantages of the lock box system are 1) the portable model requires an entrance door knob and won't work with a lever type door handle and 2) the permanent wall mount style often cannot be used for a condominium where all exterior services are common area. Pictured next are examples of the types of locks that I found to be quite convenient in a backup or emergency capacity.

Frequently Asked Questions about Access Locks

Q: Is any special door preparation required for a keyless code lock access installation? My locksmith says that a special "plate" is required to cover an existing deadbolt hole. What is he talking about?

A: On a standard prep these larger locks should cover both holes, however not all preps are standard such as with widely spaced preexisting holes or with hollow doors. In some cases, you will need a wrap-around (such as the one pictured next) that is prepped for the specific lock you select.

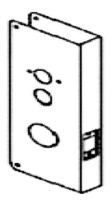

Q: The lock that I am considering apparently does not have a stainless steel facade, but rather a dull chrome finish. How do you think this will stand up in a salt air environment?

A: The dull chrome finish holds up well in challenging conditions, but keep in mind that salt will eventually get to anything.

Q: There are more expensive locks listed that advertise a "passage" function. Do I need to consider these?

A: Not really unless you plan long periods of intensive unsecured access. The "passage" function allows the lock to be set so as not to require a code at all, such as when remodeling, etc.

Q: Some locks come with at least two keys. The use of the keys will not otherwise disable the lock, correct?

A: The keys are often simply a bypass to override the buttons and usually will not otherwise interfere with the lock.

Q: What is the typical warranty period on a new lock?

A: Some manufacturers such as Simplex provide a 3 year warranty, but warranties vary.

Guest Safety and Accident Prevention

Thinking ahead is the principle requirement for achieving many owner objectives, and this is especially true when it comes to guest and home safety. Focusing on guest well being pays dividends in guest relations and liability reduction. Several areas for your consideration are presented below:

◊ **Child Proofing**
◊ **Fire Safety**

◊ **Liability Reduction**

◊ **Establishing Local Contacts**

◊ **Controlling Mail and Newspapers**

◊ **Remote Security and Monitoring**

◊ **Posted Information**

Child Proofing

Children are always my first concern. Do a "child safety survey" of your home. Try to imagine what could go wrong so that you can address it now and not have to worry about it later.

No chemicals or poisons! I like to encourage guests to clean up after themselves and many do, but I am not going to leave caustic materials anywhere in the home. Of course, I have no problem with leaving brushes and brooms and mops! Cover electrical outlets, remove dangling cords from blinds, and consider having a first aid kit available for minor emergencies, placed in clear view. I recommend that you make certain that emergency numbers, including poison control at the CDC, are posted prominently. Be sure that any cleaning or other chemical supplies are secured and beyond the reach of little hands. Do not leave fertilizers or other yard chemicals in an accessible place. Check your decks and porches to be certain that there is no hidden danger for children from falls. If either decks or porches are elevated or overhang a hard surface, I encourage you to ensure that side rails are sufficiently spaced to prevent a small child from getting through. If you have any concern, install a wire mesh or more closely spaced rails to prevent this from happening. In short, be vigilant about anticipating safety issues for all your guests, but especially for children.

Fire Safety

Earlier we discussed the need to make a policy decision about whether or not to permit smoking. Depending on the specifics of your rental home, the risk of fire could be a crucial deciding factor. My beach home in particular was located in a high fire risk area. Therefore, I did not permit smoking in the home but realized that I could not control outside smoking. Since my home was surrounded by pine straw, I was always concerned about fire. My remedy was to provide lots of ashtrays, fire warning information, fire extinguishers prominently located throughout the home and a water hose near the deck and at the ready.

It is essential to have smoke alarms, CO (carbon monoxide) detectors and fire extinguishers available on every floor near potential flash points and in prominent view. In determining the need for CO detectors, consider any appliances fueled by natural gas or propane which may be located inside the home. Also, be sure to leave extra 9 volt batteries in your owner's closet for your detectors and ensure that the batteries are changed regularly.

Liability Reduction

Aside from having the right safety equipment available, I suggest that you follow up you child safety survey with one for the adults. Tour your home and specifically look for anything that may translate into a hazard for your guests. Make certain that you have adequate lighting, especially near steps or where the floor elevation changes. Sharp, hard corners on tables or shelves, loose or slippery rugs, cracked or broken dishware, weak or splintered steps, decks, boardwalks or fences, anything that could and should be repaired, removed or replaced should be. Non slip floor surfaces and safety glass remove a lot of potential liability from the home - special attention should be given to the bath and kitchen areas where wet surfaces occur. Use non-slip mats or decals on the tub and shower floors. If you do not already have GFI outlets around your bath and kitchen sinks, have them installed. Repair lamps with worn switches, electrical outlets that cause problems, wall switches that don't perform correctly, etc. Examine your kitchen knives; this is the one area that I DON"T recommend having the newest and the best! Razor sharp, new technology knives are probably too dangerous for a rental home.

Establishing Local Contacts

You will find it useful to establish contacts and relationships with neighbors, police, regime management employees, local business people, etc. I encourage you to network as much as possible, particularly with your neighbors. Tell them about your rental program, give them your contact information, be receptive to their issues, complaints and ideas, and encourage them to contact you if they have concerns or notice anything unusual.

Controlling Mail and Newspapers

Most owners do not receive mail or newspaper delivery at their rental property. Some, however, do wish to receive local mail and/or newspapers since they use their home as a residence some portion of the year or they decide to provide newspapers as an amenity to their guests. In this circumstance, I recommend establishing a local PO or contract post box where mail can be received and forwarded according to your instructions. In this manner, you are relieved of the burden of temporary forwarding of mail, address changes or confusion at the post office. If you have papers delivered to your door (as I do), don't forget to put them on hold if you are away. You should be given credit toward future deliveries.

Remote Security and Monitoring

Even though they are uncommon, floods, storms and fires are the worst fears of people with vacation properties located far away from where they live. Technology is now available to monitor and control your vacation rental property from a distance if you so desire. You may either use a contracted security monitoring service, or set up your own video surveillance system to monitor your home over the internet. Though I do not specifically recommend this level of security, it is important that you understand your options.

Posted Information

After you have considered all of the above, inform your guests of safety issues by posting information on all safety considerations and other critical information. Remind them of the 911 service and include the home's address and phone number in the same vicinity - responders usually need this information. Post in a prominent place, such as on your refrigerator door or a cabinet near the telephone.

Addressing Storage Issues

Different types of storage will be required at your vacation rental home in order to meet both owner and renter needs. You will recall that earlier I suggested that you start to think about your storage requirements and to proceed to make the necessary adjustments. What works in your home will largely be a balance between what you ideally would like to have and what your home can physically accommodate. Your renters will rightfully expect sufficient usable closet space sufficient for their temporary visit; this sometimes dictates how much space is left to meet personal storage needs. Let's cover some basic interior storage issues.

◊ **Storage Keys vs. Code Locks**

◊ **Owner Closets**

◊ **Cleaning Closets**

◊ **Kitchen Closets**

◊ **Guest Safe**

◊ **Supplemental Owner Closets**

◊ **Exterior Utility Storage**

Storage Keys vs. Code Locks

Your overall storage plan should consider which storage closets should be keyed alike and which keyed separately. For instance, using separately keyed locks will enable you to provide cleaning closet access without compromising the integrity of your personal closet. On the other hand, if you have several closets intended to be accessed only by the owner, you will find it convenient to key these closets alike.

Most owners simply provide interior closet door keys to all cleaning and maintenance personnel. In most instances, a keyed door handle lock will work fine. The principal problem with this is of course that keys can get lost or misplaced, which can be a real problem if an emergency arises and you don't have a backup plan. If many different individuals will be accessing the home for services, an alternative arrangement similar to the exterior lock boxes described previously is excellent: keys to cleaning closets are permanently stored on premise in code lock accessible boxes and the codes are easily shared. The advantages of using code activated lock boxes for interior service closets are similar to those sited for exterior access doors. Finally, if you want to ensure that your closets remain secure, be certain to consider installing readily available security hinges that cannot be removed from the outside.

Owner Closets

You will want to setup, at a minimum, one personal closet. There are innumerable things like supplies, clothes, toiletries, etc. that you may wish to keep on-site so that they will be there when you need them, where you need them. The primary owner's closet is typically located in the master bedroom, but that of course depends on where you have space. If you use your home a lot, you might enjoy doing what I did. I added a small refrigerator in my owner's closet in order to keep condiments, cold drinks and other perishable items ready for my return! Of course, I had to install a light and an electrical outlet to accommodate my needs, but this was not a huge problem.

Cleaning Closets

You may also choose to setup a cleaning closet if you want to assist your cleaning person by keeping cleaning supplies, guest starter supplies, extra bed linens, towels, etc. on hand. This may depend on your arrangement with your housekeeper since many insist on bringing everything with them on every cleaning visit. The cleaning closet was critical for me at both my vacation rental homes since I wanted access to these supplies when I was in residence as well as having them available for the cleaning person. I typically installed shelves in all of my storage closets in order to take full advantage of my available space.

Owner's Pantry

In homes that have sufficient kitchen storage space, generally cabinets, you might find it fun and helpful to setup a locked "owner's pantry" in order to store nonperishable foods and kitchen supplies that you want to have available when you visit. An owner's pantry may enable you to reduce the size of your main owner's closet, and is certainly handier to access for items needed in the kitchen.

Guest Safe

No one likes to think about dealing with crime while on vacation, but reality sometimes intrudes. Thieves do strike anywhere and everywhere and people on vacation can make good targets. In a resort community during the rental season, everybody is accustomed to seeing strangers and thieves blend in easily. Renters frequently are away from the home for long periods and leave things like jewelry, cell phones, consumer electronics and even laptop computers behind. For this reason, even the nicest hotels provide safes for their guests to store particularly valuable items, so you might consider this as well. Built-in wall or floor safes or even free standing safes that are secured to the home can be a lifesaver for your guests who are away from their home and dependent on your foresight. Be sure to purchase the type of safe made for this application that allows guests to set their own combinations, typically four digit codes. These safes also include a master code which can be used to open the safe at any time in the event of a problem.

Supplemental Owner Closets

Maybe you can cram everything into your owner's closet but, if you have the space, you may benefit from a second utility closet. This is especially important for owners who do their own repairs in order to store such things as tools and equipment out of the sight and reach of visitors. You can also expect any of your personal sports equipment that is not stored in a secure location to be used and misplaced by renters so it is important to consider this as well. Beach umbrellas, chairs, coolers and the like for beach home owners; skies, poles, boots, sleds, etc. for ski destinations, etc.

Exterior Utility Storage

If you have a standalone residence and are not in a condo, the answer to your storage problem may be found outside of the home. My solution for yard maintenance equipment and outdoor supplies was always simple and very much a function of the home itself. I was not too concerned with security as much as I was with getting things put out of sight. In one case, the space underneath my deck was used for tools and, in another, the home was built in such a way as to provide ample, semi weather protected storage underneath the home. If you have a large yard, you can easily build a storage shed to accommodate all your outside storage needs. As long as weather damage or theft is not an issue and assuming that we are not talking about dangerous items, outside storage is just fine.

Home Inventory and Setup

Properly preparing your home is critical to renter satisfaction and rental program success. Plus, for those who are meticulous about their home, getting it set up just right is very rewarding! In fact, chances are that you have already provided for most of the items that we will discuss in this section if you have rented your home before. In any case, I suggest that you review the information that follows to be certain that you aren't missing some small but important item that most people take for granted and depend on. Guests notice when a property owner has anticipated commonly used conveniences. Let's review some of the things that you should consider when furnishing and stocking your home.

◊ **Starter Supplies**
◊ **Telephone Restrictions**
◊ **Covering the Basics**

◊ **Furniture and Furnishings**

◊ **Sleeping Arrangements**

◊ **Kitchen Appliances and Utensils**

◊ **Decks and Porches**

◊ **Thermostat Settings**

◊ **Final Quality Check**

Starter Supplies

When you check into a hotel, you expect that a few basic items will be available in case you have forgotten to pack an essential. It is no different with your guests and your vacation home. Typically your renters will arrive late in the day and not take time to visit the grocery store until the next day. A few inexpensive items stocked in the home may make their first night infinitely more comfortable. For a typical rental home, the basics that you might consider, your "starter supplies", should include the following:

Bathroom

◊ **Toilet Paper** - Be sure to have each bathroom prepared for your guest's late day arrival! The cost is minimal so add an extra roll or two somewhere in the home.

◊ **Small Soaps** - A small soap in each bathroom will help to ensure that your guests do not come up short if they choose to bathe before they make a trip to the store. The little oatmeal soaps are very cool and inexpensive!

◊ **Small Lotions and Shampoos** – Skin lotion and baby shampoo is all that is needed to provide a starter supply of bathroom body essentials.

Kitchen

◊ **Paper Towels** - A roll of paper towels in the kitchen will buy a little extra time for your guests to do their own shopping for the week.

◊ **Trash Bags** - This is as much for you as it is for your guests! Anything that you can do to increase sanitation in your home will pay dividends for both you and your renters.

◊ **Dish Washer Detergent** – Just enough detergent for one load is all that is needed to avoid guest frustration.

Telephone Restrictions

Although cell phones are quickly becoming a viable replacement for land lines, most owners choose to provide a land line telephone in their rental home for guest convenience. After all, you can't assume that the guest cell phone will work locally or, for that matter, that they even have a cell phone. If you do have a land line telephone in the home, you need to be certain to contact your service provider and restrict the use of the line to local calls and toll free dialing. Most providers offer a plan to accommodate this goal, albeit at some nominal charge. In addition to blocking normal long distance service, be sure to consider 900 numbers, incoming collect calls, information calls (411) and any other potential sources of abuse. Discuss your needs with the providers agent and make certain your have covered all of your exposures. Keep in mind that some guests may want to use a calling card for long distance which requires you to permit access to 800 or 888 area codes.

Covering the Basics

Air Conditioning and Heat - I'm sure that you will make do with whatever you have in your home in regards to your HVAC system as long as it is functional. I will caution you, however, not to push an old system too long. As a landlord, you are responsible for providing reasonably comfortable living conditions and that certainly includes heat in the cold periods and air conditioning in the hot months - in most cases, you are legally liable for your guest's wellbeing while they are in the home. The downside of an HVAC breakdown in midseason is very bad. You must RUSH to make what is an expensive repair under the best of circumstances and will more likely pay a premium to get the work done quickly. Even so, you are not likely to get the repair done quickly enough to salvage the rental, so you can expect to refund the rent amount or pay for alternative housing for your guest. And lastly, your guests are bound to be unhappy and unlikely to return. With so much at stake, don't put off needed repairs or replacements too long.

Major Appliances - The same can be said for your major appliances – you can't really afford a failure if you rent your home to others! What might suffice if only you or your family were to be inconvenienced becomes a major problem if you have renters in the home. Be sure that your refrigerator, stove, dishwasher, microwave and hot water heater are in good condition before you advertise your home for rent. And do yourself a favor – no glass top appliances.

High-capacity Washer and Dryer - If you are purchasing a washer or dryer for your home, be sure to get the heavy duty, high capacity models. The wear and tear on these appliances will likely be substantial, especially if your housekeeper relies on them to do the weekly laundry between guests. And in many situations, you or your renters will be laundering beach towels or frequent loads during stays at the home. Money spent on these critical appliances will be well worth the cost.

Furniture and Furnishings

Furniture - Comfort and durability are tops on my list for a rental home. Select furniture with upholstery that will stand up to frequent use. Either have your new furniture treated for stain prevention at the store or treat it yourself as soon as it is delivered. You can do your own pre treatment for stain prevention at very little cost.

Carpets - If you replace carpets, selecting a type that offers wear and stain resistance is very important. The carpet that I had in my mountain home was the best I ever had in a rental home. It was a tight pile (Berber) with a speckled color scheme that hid dirt and stains and was easily cleaned.

Dining Room Seating Capacity - If you advertise your home as suitable for ten people, then you need to be certain that your eating and seating arrangements accommodate the advertised number of guests. If your home can sleep 12 people, you don't necessarily have to have one gigantic table, but may choose to include your bar as part of your seating plan. Certainly include TV trays in the home if you wish, but I would not count them as a part of your planned capacity.

Lighting - Plenty of good quality lighting is essential to both guest enjoyment and safety. Consider where they will work and play. I liked to have lots of lamps because they added to the ambiance and because they could be scattered around every corner of the home.

Sleeping Arrangements

One of the most important decisions that a rental homeowner makes is how to set up the beds in the home. Your sleeping options will determine who you can market to, how many people you can accommodate and who is likely to rent your home. For instance, if you are marketing your property to golfers, you're usually better off if you don't expect them to share a double bed! Of course, your home will largely dictate what you can do, but you may have some discretion also.

Always select queen size beds over doubles if the room sizes can accommodate them. Tall guests simply won't be comfortable in anything less. If you have a large master bedroom, a king size bed might give you an edge over the competition, but I would discourage you from crowding a room with an overly large bed. If you decide that the best solution for a small third or fourth bedroom is singles or even bunk beds, be sure to make that clear to your potential renters. I like the idea of including a comfortable sleeper sofa in my home to accommodate a larger rental group, but make sure that your advertised sleeping arrangements point this out.

Kitchen Appliances and Utensils

Ice maker - Ice makers are popular with guests, not only for convenience but also for the "no hands" sanitation benefits if you have an in-door dispenser. Be prepared for service calls since maintenance is frequently an issue.

Kitchen Linens - Dish towels, dish cloths, hot pads, place mats and tablecloths when appropriate. The latter two items are much better in vinyl than cloth in a rental home.

Small Kitchen Appliances - Toaster, can opener, coffee maker, blender and any other small specialty appliance that you don't mind having to clean every week. I say no countertop ovens - I just don't trust them for fire safety reasons.

Kitchen Utensils and Supplies - Flatware, corkscrew, spatula(s), serving spoons, bottle openers (mounted is great), measuring cups, colander, vegetable peeler, scissors, microwave containers. This stuff is cheap at Dollar Tree but very important to renter happiness!

Dinnerware and Glassware - Sturdy equals safe in glassware. Be sure to include wine and cocktail glasses. Dinnerware should be microwave safe, (no stoneware) and include serving bowls.

Pots and Pans - Stock a full variety of pots and pans. Many owners prefer stainless steel to handle the wear and tear. Non-stick cookware just won't hold up to the rental crowd. Even though they will occasionally need to be replaced, I do suggest a couple of non stick skillets.

Coolers - Provide a couple of plastic coolers marked with the home address for your guests to use on trips to the beach or picnics anywhere.

Cooking Spices - A new spice rack will be very popular with your gourmet cooking guests.

Electric Grill - If you have the countertop space, I suggest that you add one of the electric grills that have become so popular in recent years. I am a little bit of a grilling snob, but I have to admit I was pleasantly surprised at the results when I used one for the first time. An inside grill is especially welcome if your home is not equipped for outdoor grilling.

Decks and Porches

I love homes and condos with decks and porches and so do guests! I don't see how you can expect people who smoke not to escape to the porch for a cigarette, so you might as well prepare for that eventuality with a suitable spot and an available ashtray. In some areas and seasons, screened porches are a necessity in order for you guests to avoid bugs and still enjoy your outside living space. These areas can become a highlight of their stay if you take the time and expense to furnish and maintain them properly.

> *If you have the space and infrastructure to support them, I can't encourage you enough to include swings and hammocks, table and chairs, chase lounges, and anything similar that enables your guests to enjoy the outdoors.*

Thermostat Settings

In hot climates, I suggest leaving the thermostat at 80-85 degrees during the summer when the unit is vacant to help control moisture. For owners of properties that experience cold weather, I suggest leaving the thermostat set at 55 when the unit is vacant just to be certain that inside temperatures don't ever get to freezing.

Final Quality Check

As a final review, consider those aspects of your rental home that make the strongest impression on your guests. *Take a look at the following checklist, think about which areas offer the most potential for improvement with your property and start now to consider what you would like to do to improve your home's "customer appeal".*

- Is your home clean?
- Does it smell good when you walk in?
- Do you have comfortable beds?
- Is your furniture reasonably attractive?
- Are shelves and countertops uncluttered?
- Does it look freshly painted?
- Are all appliances in good condition?
- Have you repaired all damaged or broken items?
- Is your kitchen fully stocked?
- Are your linens comfortable and new looking?

- Is your bug treatment effective?

- Do your carpets and floors look and feel clean?

- Does your exterior appear to be well kept?

- Are clear written information and instructions posted?

If you can answer "yes" to all of these questions, you are well ahead in the battle for your renter's loyalty and satisfaction!

Chapter 8

From Good to Great!

Happy renters are returning renters and nothing is appreciated more by your guests than finding a comfortable home prepared in advance for their vacation enjoyment. Use your imagination and consider these suggestions to increase the appeal and comfort of your home. Your guests will also be happy about information and equipment that they can use to pursue outdoor adventures in good weather or a home stocked with books, movies and games for days when indoor activities are their only option. With a little foresight and effort you can do a lot to ensure a memorable guest experience!

- **Increasing Appeal and Comfort**
- **Fun When the Sun is Shining**
- **Activities for Bad Weather Days**

Increasing Appeal and Comfort

After you have prepared for the rental process, it's time to use your imagination to enhance the appeal of your home and the comfort of your guests. I say imagination because there is really no limit to what you can do to provide extra enjoyment and satisfaction for your renters. Your preparation will result in enhancements which can be used both to promote your home to potential renters and to make those who choose your home for their stay want to come back and recommend your home to others. Some enhancements may be expensive, while others are more a matter of effort and attention to detail. No one knows your home and the opportunities it presents better than you do, but here are a few ideas for your consideration.

◊ **Invest in Quality**
◊ **Convenience Features**
◊ **Grills and Grilling**
◊ **Extra Extras**

Invest in Quality

An investment in quality and durability is smart because it is almost always cost effective in a rental home. You will save money with less frequent replacement and repair costs, time and effort in replacing broken or worn out fixtures and appliances and guest unhappiness with broken or dilapidated fixtures. When you are weighing your purchase decision, also keep in mind the positive impression that it makes on your guests when they arrive to find quality appliances and furniture in the home. Remember that your guest's good feelings often translate into return renters!

Convenience Features

Hairdryers - I installed hairdryers in every bathroom of the homes I owned. They were cheap, appreciated and gave me something else to pitch in my home description. Be sure to include toilet brushes in every bath in the home so that your guests can help with their own maintenance. Clean and functional are the key ingredients with bathrooms.

Handheld Showers - You may or may not choose to outfit your showers with these convenient add-ons, but they are important for some "vertically challenged" guests, and essential for many disabled people. If you decide to up fit your home for handicapped access, handheld showers are a part of the formula.

Hand Soap Dispensers - The little soap dispensers are great for hand washing. No soap is wasted and they are completely reusable from one guest to the next since they are sanitary. I liked to buy a large refill and asked my housekeeper to refill the dispensers when they got low. Inexpensive and convenient!

Handheld Vacuums - This is another one of those ideas that is helpful for your guests <u>and</u> good for your home. I suggest that you locate one on every floor.

Alarm and Common Area Clocks - Every bedroom should have an alarm clock, and common areas such as the kitchen and den should have wall clocks that are easy to read.

Digital Answering Machine - Be sure and get the digital variety for reliability and ease of use. Put a copy of the instructions nearby, and keep a copy in your owner's closet since you will need to reprogram it occasionally. I suggest that you program a generic greeting giving the home address and resort name. That way anybody who calls knows that they are leaving the message at the correct address.

Grills and Grilling

I was fortunate that I was allowed to grill at both my homes since I loved it, my guests loved it and I could include it in my promotional material. I used propane which I felt was much safer than charcoal. If you don't provide a grill, be sure to tell your visitors that charcoal is not allowed for fire safety reasons. The challenge for me was the propane fuel supply. I solved my problem by having two propane tanks and coaching my visitors to not go dry before they filled the empty tank. I worked hard from the beginning to make certain that they understood that propane refills were their responsibility and was careful to tell them where to find the most convenient propane refill station. Whenever I visited the home, I always filled both tanks. With a little luck, a couple of tanks of fuel could last through a month or more of renters.

You have to know and follow the rules for grilling whether they come from your policy, neighborhood covenants or local ordinances. If guests are not allowed to grill outside of your home, don't keep it a secret from them but do provide them with a large countertop electric grill. Those things work pretty good as an alternative to having nothing!

Extra Extras

Welcome Basket - Some people are big on welcome baskets and I guess they are another nice touch if you are local to your rental home and want to handle this yourself. I personally wouldn't ask my housekeeper to take responsibility for this – they have enough to do.

Drinking Water Filtration - Depending on the water quality available to your home, you might want to consider an inexpensive filtration system. Even with good water quality, visitors might be accustomed to water that has a different flavor than that available in your home and, if so, will appreciate your extra effort in accommodating their tastes. This can be particular issue for beach area homes since the water usually has a distinctive taste. Under counter solutions are not expensive, although filters will have to be changed occasionally.

Wines - Here's one I bet you never thought of. I used to keep a six bottle wine rack in my mountain house on a kitchen shelf. I left a note nearby encouraging visitors to help themselves to the wine, requesting only that they replace in kind. Most did! Plus, you wouldn't believe the nice comments that I received from departing guests about the whole idea. There is something friendly and trusting about it that my guests really appreciated.

Decorating and Décor - Whether you hire a professional decorator or do it yourself, the décor of the home is an important reflection of you. Many readers are quite expert at home decorating so I won't presume to lecture on this subject. The only thing that I will say is that, for a resort home, consider a motif that highlights what the area has to offer. In my beach home I found some great paintings of beach and inlet scenes, and in the mountain house I hung old skis on the foyer wall and an elevation map of the whole area in a bedroom. In my opinion, generic decor is fine but, for short term visitors, you can't beat a thematic design.

Fun in the Sun!

Your guests will always appreciate your efforts to enhance their vacation experience. ***Outfitting your home in a manner that increases your guests' enjoyment of the outdoors is an important part of your preparation.*** While there may be physical limitations on what you can provide, I encourage you to think through all of your options and to do the best you can to set up those amenities that maximize guest appeal. The things that you enjoy are probably the same things that your guests will appreciate, so get busy adding those features that make the most sense for your home and your environment.

Recreational Equipment

Regardless of where your home is located, there are probably area activities that require some basic equipment. If you are near the ocean, you can bet that your visitors will appreciate access to a beach umbrella and chairs, boogie boards, inner tubes and beach games. Other inexpensive sport and game equipment like badminton, volleyball and net, horseshoes and sports balls of all kinds will also add to the guest experience. Sure, you may have to replace an item or two every season, but these items are cheap to purchase and can save your guests a substantial amount in rental fees. In the mountains, I like the idea of providing binoculars for checking out the view or a telescope for star gazing. In snowy areas, sleds are great for the kids.

Outdoor Furniture

Yard - If you have a full size home with a yard, you can consider having an outside sitting area. Adirondack chairs are durable and attractive and make a great outdoor addition. A picnic table is another idea that has the dual advantage of guest enjoyment and taking the eating mess outside!

Deck and Porch - You may be one of the lucky homeowners who have a deck or screened porch. Make the most of these features by providing all the right furniture so that your guests may enjoy your outside environment.

Hammock - A hammock is a wonderful addition in almost every rental circumstance. Whether on the deck or in the yard, guests will remember this extra!

Porch Swing - It may be a bit old fashioned, but guests love a porch swing for relaxation. Rocking chairs are also a great way for guests to kick back, relax and enjoy the sun and breezes.

Swimming Pool

Your home either has a pool or it doesn't. Of course, you may have access to a shared pool also. Either way, this amenity should be featured prominently in your advertising. The upside is obvious, but pool owners will quickly tell you that there are extensive maintenance and safety issues involved.

While many homeowners elect to handle their own pool maintenance, this is not an option for absentee owners who rent their homes to visitors. Contracted pool maintenance isn't cheap, but it is the only option that makes sense for an absentee landlord, regardless of whether you manage your own rental program or use a property management firm.

A bigger related issue for many rental owners is when there is a community or resort pool for which membership is required. Whether or not you join and pay the cost of membership depends on a number of things, including the cost, other swimming options, what the competition is offering, etc. A word of caution: be sure that you are candid and clear in your advertising what renters will be entitled to. You won't come out ahead if you save money but end up with rental guests who feel that they have been mislead.

Outdoor Hot Tub

This is a super benefit to have in your home or on your deck! In a mountain setting, many people shop specifically for this feature when choosing their vacation home. But there are some serious sanitation issues: I can't even repeat some of the stories I've heard about how these tubs are used and abused. Believe it or not, some owners even cover their hot tubs when they rent their homes! Talk to a hot tub dealer about what is required in terms of regular professional service and sanitation procedures. It isn't that it can't be managed, it's just that it will cost something.

Outdoor Showers

If you don't already have an outside shower, you might want to consider installing one for several reasons. First, they don't cost that much to install since the plumbing is above ground. Second, they are a major convenience for both you and your guests when coming in from yard work or outdoor activities, especially when returning from the beach when everybody is covered with sand. And third, leaving the heavy soil outside will save lots of wear and tear and cleaning on your carpets, floors and furniture. They also come in handy for washing yard tools and pets!

Activities for Bad Weather Days

One thing that was extremely well received by my guests was the emphasis that I placed on providing for indoor alternatives that the renting families could enjoy when the weather was not conducive to outdoor recreation. ***It is a simple matter to think about and incorporate indoor "entertainment appeal" into your home***. Potential renters will love your emphasis on the extras! There will be times when inclement weather will impact your guests; after all, it rains everywhere sooner or later! A modest effort to anticipate some "down time" and to provide guest activity alternatives will really pay off. Here is a partial list of entertainment related items that you will want to consider as you prepare your home for renters.

Televisions

I was always big on including a TV in every bedroom in addition to the main room. This gives the guests so much more opportunity for a little privacy on that long week with the in-laws! If you are going to market amenities, you should probably start by having a large, high quality flat screen TV in the principal living area or family room. There are some dedicated sports fans that will require a great TV before they will even commit to renting a home and who make it a key search criteria. Big sports fans might not necessarily want to have to retreat to a local sports bar in order to watch their favorite sporting event.

Cable Service

A subscription to extended cable service is a necessity because it is generally expected by guests. In addition, you should consider providing premium channels for your guests such as HBO or special interest channels that have wide appeal, like dedicated sports or movie channels.

DVD/VHS Players

I like the idea of having a DVD player in every room along with the TV. If you have space limitations, you might consider a combination TV/DVD player. The downside is that if one component breaks down, the entire appliance is worthless, but the space savings might dictate this approach. Another alternative to save space is to install wall mounts for your TVs – just watch out for the headroom!

Music

Don't overlook the appeal that music options will have to music lovers. Providing CDs, stereos or radios in all the rooms offers individual options for your guests, as well as increasing privacy. I don't recommend portable CD players, or "boom boxes" as they are often called, since they are easily damaged from trips to the beach or outside the home, plus they can be (inadvertently) taken when the guests depart.

Movies

A supply of movie DVDs for guests, especially children's movies, can be a good investment in guest satisfaction. I suggest that you also provide information on local movie rental options such as directions and distances so that guests may make their own viewing choices.

Computer and Internet

Consider installing a wireless internet connection for your guests and be sure to include instructions on how to connect and what to do in case the connection is not working. Including a wireless internet connection in your promotional materials may garner attention and make a big difference to some renters. Guests may want to bring their laptop computers when they visit and many of them want to be able to connect to the internet either for work or pleasure. I suggest that you set your rental home system up as a secured network and leave the ID and Password in the home just to keep outside traffic off of the system.

Board and Card Games

Games in the home are appreciated by renters because they bring families together for a group activity that is fun and fulfilling. The cost of games and a couple of decks of cards is minimal. Think what an investment of $150 would do!

Books

Many owners have accumulated books over the years that have been read and are just looking for a new home. I suggest your rental property! Reading for some people is something that they would only consider while on vacation, but is a source of great enjoyment when the time is right. Include old paperbacks, classics, children's books, anything that you can get your hands on. An advantage of books is that they seldom have to be replaced as do cards and games from which playing pieces are invariably lost.

Toys

If you decide to provide toys for the kids, be sure to look for things that are safe, not easily lost or broken and appropriate for specific age groups. Large plastic trucks and cars, for instance, are superior to models or matchbox cars.

Electronic Games

Nintendo Playstation or Sony Xbox consoles are very popular these days, of course, but be aware that you may be treading on thin ice with parents who are fed up with these time and attention consuming options. Nonetheless, the kids will love them and will remember your home fondly for providing this "extra".

What NOT to Supply

I include portable electronics on my list for guests to bring if they want them. Anything that lends itself to easy transport will probably not make it unscathed through the first week of rental. In addition, I expect guests to bring their own computers. There is no way I am going to risk a computer owned by me (and therefore with my internal identification) being used in an illegal or embarrassing way!

Chapter 9

Guest Information, Instructions and Postings

Sometimes the value that you add to your home for rental guests doesn't cost you a dime! This is certainly the case when it comes to information. You can transfer your familiarity with the home and the area to your guests over and over again by making a one time effort to document what you know. It is easy to take for granted how to fire up the grill or handle maintenance issues, where to find the best restaurants and sports rentals, when to put out the trash, etc. Take the time to document for your guests important area information, operating instructions and in-home postings. I'll even help by providing samples of sample documents in the *Appendix* and downloadable versions at www.examples.vhallc.com. The more you communicate with your guests, the more they will feel at ease, enjoy their visit and return.

- **Guest Information**
- **In-Home Instructions**
- **In-Home Postings**

Guest Information

In this section we will discuss the different types of information that you may beneficially prepare for your rental guests. I always prepared a book of laminated pages covering many of the below topics which I typically left on the kitchen counter. Your guests will appreciate your attention to detail.

◊ **General Home Information**

◊ **Restaurants**

◊ **Area Activities**

◊ **Local Vacation Resources**

◊ **Reference Materials**

◊ **Owner Cards and Brochures**

General Home Information

The single most important information that you MUST provide for your guests is that which covers the basics of your home care and maintenance. What to do in emergencies, how to handle broken small appliances and minor repairs, when and where to look for trash collection services, explanations of locked owner areas, description of parking areas, etc. Every home has special issues and considerations that are difficult for a rental guest to pick up on without your help. Sometimes something very innocuous can be a problem.

I remember when I purchased my mountain home that it took me about a week to understand that the shower control was under the faucet! Remember, anything that you wondered about when you first bought the home and lived there is going to be something that you will want to communicate to your guests. See the Appendix for an example of a general home information document.

Restaurants

In most vacation situations, one thing that you can count on is that your guests will likely go out for dining at least once during their visit, and often they will leave the home for every meal. For some people, a vacation is not a vacation if they have to cook! ***Providing your guests with information about area restaurants can be helpful and likely will be very much appreciated.*** I suggest that you furnish a list of your favorite dining establishments, along with phone numbers and locations, in your home. Look for and accumulate newspaper and magazine reviews and include information about take out services and discount opportunities in the local area. As I illustrate in my *Appendix* example, providing little mini reviews as to type of dining, hours of operation and, importantly, some personal feedback on your experiences with the establishment is a great idea!

Area Activities

One great bonus document which you may also want to prepare in advance is a list of area activities, including telephone and website information, for your guests. This can be a fun and surprisingly informative effort! To understand area activities, start with the obvious based on your personal knowledge, then consider using Google or similar search engines to discover additional attractions in the area. In addition, the local Chamber of Commerce website can be a treasure trove of valuable links and information. You will be amazed at what you can learn by taking the time to research what your area has to offer. Your results may be sent in advance and/or placed at the home in your laminated notebook. I do both, often sending my informational document in response to inquiries as an illustration of the extra attention to detail that my guests can expect. I can guarantee that your guests will appreciate your foresight and thoughtfulness when they discover your list of area restaurants, shopping, activities, events, historical sites and other places of interest.

Local Vacation Resources

Another very helpful list that you can provide to your rental guest is information about local sources of vacation equipment and supplies. Being on vacation means that visitors will likely need or want access to all sorts of both necessary and optional items to satisfy their needs. Essentials as mundane as groceries and household supplies are going to be on everybody's list almost as soon as they arrive. Adults and teenagers alike will appreciate guidance on how to quickly and easily locate recreational equipment for purchase or rent in order for them to maximize their fun! Beach renters usually want beach chairs, umbrellas, jet skis, boats and floats to use in the water and bikes and scooters to get around on land. Mountain visitors often look for ski rentals in the winter and canoes and hiking gear in the summer to take advantage of the adventures that the high country offers. Families who travel with small children sometimes require strollers and cribs and other baby management gear. Use you time and imagination to complete a list of handy vacation resources and your guests will remember you for it.

Reference Materials

In addition to the basics, your guests will benefit from your foresight if you take the time and make the effort to provide as much information in the home as possible regarding the state, region and locality. Visitors, particularly those from far away, frequently enjoy learning as much as they can while they are in the area. There are a wide variety of resource elements that you can gather to increase your guest's general knowledge covering such diverse topics as:

◊ Resort information

◊ Area street maps

◊ Trails and parks

◊ State and local guide books

◊ Local history information

◊ Tour brochures

◊ Historical sites

◊ Local wildlife information

Owner Cards and Brochures

Another one of the advantages that self managers enjoy is that they may promote their home continuously! *I like the idea of leaving promotional brochures and contact cards in the home that my renters may conveniently take with them for future reference and referrals*. Assuming that they enjoy their stay in you home, your guests will be excellent marketers for promoting your rental home to their families, friends and neighbors.

An easy and inexpensive option is to leave business cards in the home that your guests my pickup and take with them. I preferred including the address of my personal web page on the cards – I don't recommend strictly relying on telephone numbers since these may change and you do want your contact info to be good for as long as possible. A word of caution: don't leave the cards near a telephone or you'll find that they all get used to take messages!

If you are willing to go to a little trouble, consider printing short brochures highlighting all the best features of your home. Your guests can take them upon departure and share them with others to further your promotion efforts.

In-Home Instructions

Providing your visitors with carefully spelled out guidance will save everyone time, frustration and money. My experience is that my rental guests would consistently try to understand and follow through on any requests that I left for them, and I know they appreciated my help in operating household gadgets and appliances like the grill and fireplace. After all, they can't cooperate unless they know what your expectations are! Every home has little eccentricities that are only difficult to handle if they aren't understood. The list below is by no means exhaustive, but will give you a starting point.

◊ **Fire Prevention Instructions**

◊ **Departure Instructions**

◊ **Grill Instructions**

◊ **Fireplace Instructions**

◊ **Propane Instructions**

Fire Prevention Instructions

In many rental situations, the single biggest hazard to both your home and your guests is the possibility of fire. This elevated risk may result from a combination of factors including lack of familiarity with the home and appliances, reduced awareness of the dangers in the unfamiliar environment, confusion about where fire extinguishers are located, and even carelessness due to a "party" atmosphere. It is the owner's responsibility to make certain that as much information as possible is available to guests so that they are aware of the general risks and their fire prevention responsibilities. Take the time to put together a page of instructions to include in your homeowners manual to inform and educate your visitors on the dangers of fire in your community, what specific cautions that they should take to reduce the risk of fire, where extinguishers and water hoses are located and policies regarding smoking and candles. I have included an example of my instructions in the *Appendix*, but you will tailor your document specifically for your home.

Departure Instructions

One way to save yourself and your housekeeper some work is to let your guests help! *I found that most people who rented my homes were anxious to leave the home in good condition and were very willing to cooperate by complying with some basic requests*. Reminding renters of departure times helps to ensure that they are out of the housekeeper's way. Tardy departures are a real headache on days when you have back-to-back rentals. If will help greatly to ensure that such things as pool passes and keys are not misplaced if you remind guests where to put them before they depart. Otherwise, there is a good chance these things could be headed home with your visitors! You will also want to help your guests to know what to do with soiled laundry, dirty dishes and household garbage before they leave. This is especially important if there is much time between guest departure and cleaning crew arrival. Dirty laundry and dishes can encourage bugs and stink up the place if left untouched for extended periods.

Grill, Fireplace and Propane Instructions

Regardless of what particular appliances and accessories you provide to your guests, you will certainly want to help them understand the basics of their operation and safety. I have included the special instructions that I provided for one of my homes in the *Appendix*, but what you need to address may be completely different. Generally, I recommend low maintenance, "idiot proof" acessories, but even these may take a little education in order to minimize guest frustration. You will also find that your guests are much less likely to damage your home if they know the proper operation of all of its features. Refer to my examples as a starting point, then go ahead and develop precisely and carefully worded instructions for your home amenities.

In-Home Postings

In addition to leaving a countertop notebook with detailed instructions covering "how tos" in the home, I like to post key information on small laminated cards in strategic locations throughout the home. These pointed messages target high risk behavior, important responsibilities or critical information that I want my guests to be aware of. The list below gives some examples of the postings that I had in my home and may spark your thinking as to what types of posting you may require.

◊ **Telephone Numbers**
◊ **Clean Filters Posting**
◊ **Electrical Panel Layout**
◊ **No Smoking Posting**
◊ **Grill Posting**
◊ **Fireplace Posting**
◊ **Propane Posting**

These posting are pretty much self explanatory. You know your home better than anyone else so you are the best person to decide what needs to go where. The two options I used for physical presentation were a) paper printouts which I laminated and fastened to the wall or b) plastic engraved tent cards that I could place on countertops. As for subjects to address, I would just say to consider my examples in the Appendix and go from there to construct your own home posting system.

Chapter 10

Customer Service and Communications

Customer service is certainly one of the most important aspects of a self management program and an area where a private homeowner has the power and potential to really distinguish themselves and their home. We'll discuss the importance of projecting a positive customer service attitude through your communications. After that we'll cover an essential step in preparing to rent your home: the preparation of your basic rental documents i.e. lease, directions, home access instructions, etc. As with the guest documents in the previous chapter, I have provided samples of rental documents in the *Appendix* and downloadable versions at www.examples.vhallc.com. Let your personality shine through, and be an effective landlord at the same time!

- **Creating Happy Customers!**
- **Rental Documents**

Creating Happy Customers!

As far as I am concerned, creating **happy customers** is a great catchall objective for owner/managers of seasonal rental property. The advantages of happy customers are numerous: **repeat business, lower marketing costs, better care of your home, fewer complaints and subsequent referrals**. In order to have happy customers, set a positive and supportive tone from the beginning, be open and clear about your policies and consider these ideas.

◊ **Your Customer Service Attitude**

◊ **Continuous Improvement**

◊ **Exceeding Expectations**

◊ **Responding to Onsite Issues**

Your Customer Service Attitude

You project your personal image, attitude and enthusiasm every time you prepare a memo, write an email or talk to a renter over the telephone. **If you are upbeat, organized and friendly when communicating with guests and potential guests, you will find that you are far more likely to be successful.** When responding to rental inquiries, be appreciative that the inquiring person picked you and your property. They didn't have to! I like to start by simply expressing my thanks to them for their inquiry. Second, be positive and friendly even if they are asking for a time that you have clearly designated as reserved or are asking a question that will obviously NOT lead to a rental for you. People remember the small kindnesses, and someone that you have to guide elsewhere may return at a later date simply because you were helpful. Third, I like to always insert a comment about how proud I am of my home. Sure, an owner could lie, but people realize that you are unlikely to offer false assurances when you don't have to, and it can provide a great sense of comfort and confidence that your home is the right choice. Remember that just because someone calls doesn't mean that the sale is automatically going to be consummated – you should continue to sell your home's benefits on an ongoing basis. Finally, if your home is not available or is really not what they are looking for, say so and suggest other possibilities. Encourage them to inquire in the future about availability, give them the number of a local property management company with which you have had a successful relationship, or help them with their vacation planning in any way that seems appropriate. On-line renters are often first time renters and your assistance will be forever appreciated.

Continuous Improvement

Continuous improvement is a philosophy more than an activity. It is just what it sounds like: **an attitude that says that everything can be improved in some way and to some degree.** It is the opposite of being satisfied with the "status quo". It must of course be tempered by realism i.e. what makes the most sense to improve now versus what should wait until later. It is not a mandate to spend money, but rather a willingness to be proactive in the care and maintenance of your rental home. Owners with a continuous improvement attitude make the best self managers because they are always trying to make things better for their guests and for their home!

Exceeding Expectations

Total honesty with potential renters is the key to "exceeding expectations". This applies not only when responding to direct questions, but also requires that you volunteer any information that might be relevant to your potential renter whether or not they directly inquire. Excessive exaggerations are to be avoided because they only set your guests up for disappointment and are not likely to lead to happy renters. It is a great feeling to receive a call from a renter after they arrive to tell you how happy they are with the accommodations or that your home is better than they expected! If you are candid and open in your responses, the only customers that you will lose are those that would not have been happy anyway.

Responding to Onsite Issues

No matter how much you plan and prepare, the occasional issue will arise that requires a quick response from you. I keep my cell phone with me at all times in order to take action on that rare occasion when a guest has a problem that must be dealt with immediately. These issues sometimes relate to serious issues such as getting into the home upon arrival or the water is not hot, or even simple inquiries that are really not of a pressing nature. In many cases, your response is simply to make a phone call to the renter or other appropriate person and the issue is resolved. As we discussed earlier, having a reliable housekeeper and emergency maintenance contacts is the best preparation. Regardless of the nature of the inquiry, a quick and effective response will demonstrate a clear commitment to your renter's satisfaction.

Rental Documents

Preparing your primary rental documents in advance is a core responsibility and a milestone in your efforts to begin your rental program. I have included examples of recommended documents in the Appendix that you will use to communicate and contract with confirmed renters. If you wish to avoid retyping everything, you may visit www.examples.vhallc.com for downloadable WORD samples of these documents. Feel free to change these downloaded documents in any manner that you wish in order to reflect your individual circumstances. *Using the descriptions that follow and the web samples as guides, prepare rental documents specifically for your property which reflect your particular policies and procedures*. The primary documents that you should prepare in advance are as follows:

- **Introduction Letter**
- **Guest License Agreement**
- **Directions to Home**
- **Supplemental Home Access**
- **Driver Name Request**
- **Credentials**

Introduction Letter

An introduction letter will be the first correspondence that your renters receive and read from you. This is your chance to make a good impression! Welcome them and spell out the basics briefly and in as friendly and conversational tone as possible. *The objective here is to make the renter feel good about the decision that they have made in renting your home and to give a good overview of the registration and payment process.* Read my example letter in the Appendix and I am sure that you will get the idea quickly. I like to include a personal introduction, a description of the lease and payment requirements, necessary logistical arrangements (including information on home access), and some basics on what to bring to get them started. Follow-up questions from my guests are always welcome, but I realized early on that the more I included carefully thought out and worded information up front, the fewer extra inquiries I received and the more efficiently the whole rental process worked.

Guest License Agreement

Keep in mind that the license agreement example provided in the Appendix and on the web is only a sample and that your license agreement may properly contain anything that you want or be constructed in any manner that you wish. I found that I could say everything that I wished to say on a little more than a page. Also, if you read my sample, you will notice that I am very straightforward and no nonsense when it comes to spelling out the agreement. ***While I am never unfriendly in written or voice communication, my primary objective with the Guest License Agreement is to avoid misunderstandings and the problems that causes down the road.*** When you begin drafting your own document, you may want to jump ahead to the chapter on Reservations and Revenue for a discussion on establishing your payment requirements, a key policy issue. Finally, we covered the issue of seeking legal advice in an earlier chapter. If you have decided to ask someone to review your *Guest License Agreement*, do so before you go live and begin the rental process. If you are at all uncomfortable, now would be the time to put your mind at ease by seeking professional advice!

Directions to Home

Even if you take it for granted that your home is easy to locate, your guests may not be at all familiar with the area and may need your help in order to find your home when they arrive in the area. Keep in mind that they may arrive after dark or in bad weather conditions. They may also be suffering from travel fatigue and be short on energy and patience. *I like to make sure that I do everything possible to eliminate any possible problems in advance, and getting to the home for the first time can be a potential problem.* My fail safe approach is to combine turn by turn written directions (as shown by the example in the Appendix) with a link to a Map Quest type online mapping service. Encourage your renter to print out and include in their travel folder both a copy of the written directions and of a map before they ever leave home.

Home Access Detail

Some rental properties are more complicated to access than others. This is an optional document that may be prepared to address unusual or exacting circumstances with home access such as gated communities, challenging home access or parking limitations and restrictions.

Driver Name Request

Some gated communities require a check in process whereby drivers are asked for their names and these names are verified against a preapproved list before access is granted. In these situations, be prepared to gather this information for prior submission to your security personnel. Gated communities and complicated parking pass requirements sometimes necessitate a little extra effort.

Credentials

The sample *Credentials* document is optional, suitable for some but too much for others, especially if you do a good job introducing yourself in your cover letter. **If you do a good enough job with your documents and emails, you may never need to speak with your renters by phone because things will go so smoothly!**

Chapter 11

Your Rental Home on the Internet

Marketing is the centerpiece of your rental effort. In this chapter we will explain what commercial websites do, how they support your vacation home rentals and the variables that you will encounter in choosing which commercial rental websites to use. We will also address the benefits of a having a dedicated website for your home. Finally, you will write your marketing text by using our preformatted web input sample documents. Templates are located in the Appendix and on the web at www.examples.vhallc.com. Preparing your web input documents in advance will make uploading to commercial rental websites a snap!

- **Commercial Vacation Rental Sites**
- **A Website for Your Home**
- **Creating Web Input**

Commercial Vacation Rental Sites

The emergence of commercial rental websites in the mid-nineties proved to be a boon to internet savvy vacation rental home owners. Thousands upon thousands of owners and millions and millions of guests use these sites to rent vacation homes on a regular basis. This section addresses the realm of internet marketing as it pertains to vacation rental homes and condominiums. I'll discuss commercial rental websites, how they can work to assist you and the subtle (and sometimes not so subtle) differences between sites. With my guidance, you will decide how many sites you wish to utilize and how you might choose among them.

◊ **How Commercial Sites Work for You**
◊ **Commercial Web Site Features**
◊ **Selecting Your Commercial Websites**
◊ **Gauging Website Performance**
◊ **Reverse Auction Websites**

How Commercial Sites Work for You

Most commercial websites work in a similar manner. For each website on which a property is listed, homeowners typically receive a primary webpage featuring one to six main photos, and space to detail information about their property: rates, description, amenities and contact information. Your individual page is connected into the larger network by a summary listing that appears on the state, country or regional page. This geographical hierarchy ultimately leads up to the commercial site's homepage. From a potential renter's point of view, the search process is essentially in reverse order: site visitors typically drill down to your home either geographically or through a feature search.

Commercial Web Site Features

There are literally hundreds of choices in commercial websites to choose from. ***Based on my experience, some sites are a waste of money while others are very productive.*** You should assume an average cost per year of $150 - $200 per site per year to be conservative in your budgeting, although the actual cost will often be less. Most commercial sites offer added cost options such as additional pictures or listing priorities (so that your listing shows in front of other listings in the same category), as well as the opportunity to include a link to your standalone dedicated site if you have one. I recommend contracting for minimum cost options only, particularly if you have your own property website for additional pictures and information. If you decide to take advantage of some of these extra cost site features at a later date when you become more familiar with the process, by all means do so, though you may find these premium features to be unnecessary.

Selecting Your Commercial Websites

It is up to you how many sites you choose on which to list your property. ***It may come as no surprise to you when I say that the more sites the better when you are looking to build a base of rental business.*** On the contrary, you may save a little money initially by listing with only a couple of sites if, for instance, you already have a dependable core of return guests from prior experience. It is also true that fewer sites mean somewhat less ongoing effort, particularly if you make lots of rate changes, etc. However, given the relatively modest cost of additional sites compared to your overall investment of time and money, I recommend initially listing your property on at least five commercial sites, particularly if you are just starting out. In the next chapter, I will walk you through my suggested process for identifying and selecting the commercial rental web sites that you will initially use for your home. Generally, my approach is to use a combination of websites, with some selected based on their web ranking and others selected based on an assessment of the competition from other rental properties in your area.

Gauging Website Performance

Although you may choose an initial subscription term of one month to one year with most commercial sites, I recommend jumping in and doing a full year. You have to spend a little time with the setup, plus it will probably take at least a full rental season to decide if your money is being spent wisely based on the number if inquiries you receive from a given commercial subscription. This will also give you a chance to evaluate such things as the site's design and ease of use and make your own judgment call as to which subscriptions to renew and when it is time to try a different one.

Data on access to your listing by potential renters is frequently accumulated by the commercial website itself and provided to subscribers for use in analyzing traffic and contact activity. *At a minimum, try to at least gauge the relative performance of each site once each year.* You will then be in a good position to determine which and how many sites you wish to renew.

Reverse Auction Websites

There is one approach of which I am aware that is quite different from others in that they use a "reverse auction" methodology. Deciding whether or not to participate in a reverse auction web site has critical implications for you in that it requires somewhat more effort on your part than is otherwise the norm. This extra effort may be worth it for you if you have the time and really want to maximize income. The reverse auction process allows inquiring visitors to describe their desired destination, number of bedrooms, acceptable rate range, etc. in broad terms. This information is then broadcast en masse to all owners whose property even roughly matches the description. Given this approach, you will find that you get more inquiries more frequently, understanding that they are not considering your home in particular but, rather, are offering you a chance to compete for their business. In order to capture the booking, you must respond promptly, meet their specific needs and compete on price.

Deciding to subscribe to a reverse auction site is a judgment call that only you can make, primarily based on your time constraints and personal preference. ***By way of guidance, I will say that you are likely to increase your bookings by using a reverse auction website, particularly if you have a desirable home, but at a considerable cost in time and effort.*** My decision has always been that it was not worth the hassle simply because of restraints on my time and the rental success I had otherwise.

A Website for Your Home

Whether you choose to self manage or employ the services of a property management company, there are distinct advantages to having a dedicated web site for your vacation home. While it is helpful to have a home web page even if you use the rental management services of others, I would say categorically that, if you are self managing, a website specifically built for your rental home is a key competitive advantage.

◊ **Benefits of a Dedicated Website**
◊ **Contact a Website Developer**

Benefits of a Dedicated Website

The many ways in which you will benefit from your own vacation home web page include:

◊ Establish a stable point of contact and reference for your past renters even if you change email addresses or use different commercial web sites in future years.

◊ Allow interested parties to link to your property or add your home to their "favorites" without creating the necessity that they visit a commercial website.

◊ Publish multiple pictures of your home for inquisitive potential renters without having to pay for upgrades at commercial websites in order to have them post extra pictures.

◊ Present lengthy and detailed descriptions of amenities and layout without being subject to commercial web site limitations.

◊ Provide a direct link to your availability calendar for potential guests.

◊ Provide a direct link to a map to your home.

◊ Offer other helpful links to information on area attractions and activities for the convenience and information of guests and potential guests.

◊ Personalize and individualize your communication with potential renters by using an email address with a signature that publicizes your home.

◊ Anticipate and answer questions in advance by disclosing prices and policies in greater detail.

◊ Demonstrate the sense of the pride you have in your home by establishing a dedicated web site independently of any commercial listings..

> *I suggest that you have a dedicated website developed for your rental home separate from the commercial sites on which you choose to list.*

Contact a Website Developer

At this point you are ready to begin the process of developing the input documents that you will need to provide to your website developer in order for them to design and populate your web page.

> *At* www.VacationHomeAdvisors.com*, we specialize in building and hosting affordable websites for vacation rental home owners.*

Please review the chapter covering online resources for a more detailed description of our services. I suspect that there are also other companies and individuals ready, willing and (hopefully) able to create a website for you. **Whomever you** *choose to assist you, I encourage you to put this on your list of things to get done now!*

Creating Web Input

Filling Out Descriptive Information

Now that you have an understanding of how the internet can help you rent your property, it's time to **develop the specific input that your developer will use to populate your dedicated website and that you will use to input into the selected commercial sites**. I have provided sample documents in the *Appendix* and electronic versions at www.examples.vhallc.com. The nine documents are:

◊ **General Information**

◊ **Bulleted Highlights**

◊ **Long Description**

◊ **Short Description**

◊ **Home Layout**

◊ **Home Amenities**

◊ **Specific Area Attraction**

◊ **General Area Activities**

◊ **Seasonal Rental Periods, Minimum Stays and Rates**

Begin by reading through the rest of this chapter to get your first look at these documents and to understand what purpose they serve. After you have familiarized yourself, you will be ready to develop your own input documents.

Using the samples provided in the Appendix and on the web, develop customized word processing documents that reflect your home, your area, your policies and your rental

You should be able to accomplish this task based on your understanding of your home and its features and the rate information we discussed earlier.

General Information

Your rental home address and other basic information that you assemble here will be required by every website that you select. Sleeping capacity is usually a critical renter consideration, and is used by many web sites to organize and segregate listings. You must provide good and accurate information regarding your Sleep Capacity to avoid potentially disastrous misunderstandings. Provide a single capacity number or feel free to specify a range if, for instance, you have a sleeper sofa that provides extra capacity. **Examples:**

STREET ADDRESS: 9010 Willow Lane

CITY: Mt. Pleasant

COUNTY: Charleston

STATE: South Carolina

TYPE OF PROPERTY: Single family home

POLICIES: No pets please

No smoking please

CC Required for damage deposit

SLEEP CAPACITY: 10 (12 with sleeper sofa)

Bulleted Highlights

Bulleted highlights help renters focus on your best attributes at one glance. Make a list of six to ten of the most appealing things about your home. What is unique about your home? What are the things that will most likely excite interest? What is important in your vacation area?

Example Bulleted Highlights:

- **Fantastic View of Resort!**
- **Private Swimming Pool!**
- **Country Club Membership!**
- **Decks and Porches Galore!**
- **Walk to Beach!**

Long Description

A good, detailed description of your rental property can be very powerful and seductive to the potential renter. This is your chance to brag about why you are so proud of your home! In addition, this field is often searched by various search engines. Adding keywords here can be important in order for renters to find your rental listing.

Example Long Description: A beautiful three-story, four-bedroom, three-bath home with quaint Victorian Beach Cottage styling. Owner has taken the extra effort to ensure that the home meets standards beyond the expected level of comfort and convenience. Owner dedication to home upkeep and guest satisfaction is not to be overlooked when shopping on the web. Located in exclusive Summer Homes section (only 24 homes), considered to be the most appealing neighborhood in the resort. Located on cul-de-sac and with private community walk to beach ~ 200 yards. Children love this home for central location, accessibility to activities and top floor double bunk bedroom! Access to oceanfront swimming pools and across the street from golf course clubhouse.

Short Description

A carefully worded short description of six to twelve words is often the first thing potential renters see when perusing web rental listings. Cut to the chase and focus on your key property attributes with a distinctive introductory phrase.

Example Short Description: Four-bedroom, three-bath home w beach access, oceanfront pools and Fazio golf courses

Home Layout

The more information that you provide to guests about the way that your home is laid out, the more you will increase their confidence that it is the right choice for them and the higher your chances will be for a rental. While layout is not a common search field, many guests have specific preferences depending on their family or group makeup or anticipated sleeping arrangements.

Example Home Layout: Dual Master Suites. First floor: Living room, dining room, kitchen, Master bedroom (queen) with bath. Second floor: Master bedroom (king) with bath, bedroom (queen), hall bath. Third floor: Bedroom (two bunk beds/sleeps four kids)

Home Amenities

List all that your home has to offer in the way of standard, convenience and luxury features. Listing your home amenities can be very advantageous when potential renters look for specific rental property attributes or compare properties. I would put as much as possible in this section.

Example Home Amenities: Cable TV, TV/DVD player in every room w/ 50 inch Large Screen TV in family room. Stereo/CD Player in Living area. Heart Pine floors downstairs and wood blinds throughout, plus a selection of movies and books for the kids. Dual level climate controls (upstairs and down). Hair dryers in every bathroom._Over-sized screened back porch with view of lagoon and tennis courts. Large open front porch with rocking chairs, porch swing and hammock. Weber propane gas grill.

Specific Area Attractions

Many renters narrow their search to listings related to a specific attraction, activity or event in their intended destination area. Be sure to include festivals, sporting events, landmarks and areas of historical interest. It is extremely important to add the proper names of specific area attractions and activities. Hint: Call the Chamber of Commerce for a list of noteworthy area attractions or events.

Example Specific Area Attractions: Ridgetop Resort Community, Scottish Summer Festival, Access to Oceanside Resort Pools and Grill, Metropolitan Museum, Riverbanks Historic Area, Tom Fazio Golf Course, Hampton Plantation Tours, Oceanside City Aquarium, USS Ohio, etc.

General Area Activities

This is where you develop an appealing list of all the various activities in which your guests may indulge during their visit. Focus on really selling the community and surrounding area! The more extensive the list, the more you can engage their imaginations. You never know what will appeal to a particular guest, and highlighting a wide range of things to do will give all the members of the visiting party something to get excited about!

Example General Area Activities: **Swimming, skiing, sunbathing, sightseeing, walking tours, historical sites, museums, nightclubs, restaurants, tennis facilities, water parks, nature trails, motor bike rentals, basketball courts, kayaking, boat rentals, golf courses, offshore, pier and inlet fishing.**

Seasonal Rental Periods, Minimum Stays and Rates

By specifying a minimum stay, you will screen out unwanted inquiries. Minimums can be waived as need be or as open dates approach. For initial rates, start with your prior rates if you have rented previously, consider a small reduction for competitive advantage or go back and reread the Chapter 2 discussion on rates and occupancy. Remember that occupancy is imperative early on. You can always raise rates later if your occupancy justifies it. **Examples:**

In Season	**(1/1-2/28)**	
	Four Night Minimum	$2000
	Weekly	$2800
Spring	(4/1-5/31)	
	Weekly	$2200
Summer	(6/1-9/15)	
	Weekly	$2800
	Monthly	$8000
Fall	(9/16-10/31)	
	Weekly	$1800

Late Fall/Early Winter (11/1-12/15)

    Weekly $1600

Holidays:

    Easter Week $3000

    Thanksgiving Week $2500

    Christmas Week $3000

Notes:

    1) Cleaning/linen fee of $150 for all reservations

    2) All rates subject to 12% local and state tax

With the above customized documents completed for your home, you are now ready to cut and paste information to the commercial websites, submit information to a developer for a dedicated web page for your property and respond to rental inquiries.

Chapter 12

Time to Go Live!

This is the final step in attracting rental shoppers from the internet to your home! When all is ready, you will "go live" with a new dedicated web site for your home – an exciting and rewarding experience. At this point you are also ready to select and populate commercial rental marketing sites using the web input documents that you previously have prepared. We will also explain how to create and link an online availability calendar and guest book so that potential renters only contact you for open dates, a critical and time saving exercise. After this phase is complete, your rental home will be on-line and ready for business!

- **Your New Dedicated Web Site!**
- **Your Commercial Rental Sites**
- **Availability Calendar and Guest Book**

Your New Dedicated Web Site!

Now is the time that you have been waiting for! You have received confirmation from your developer that the dedicated web site for your vacation rental is up and running and ready to go. The first thing that you should do is to visit your new site to verify the final accuracy of all information, particularly your rental rates and seasons, the wording of your key policies and any other items that renters and potential renters will rely on when they are making their rental decision. Ultimately you are responsible for what is presented on your dedicated webpage, so you'll want to make certain that it is clear and accurate. After you have carefully studied the information on your site, alert the developer to any factual errors that need to be corrected before you refer visitors to it. Note the complete web address of your site. You will need to have it handy for posting on the commercial sites as you go through the registration process. Once you have proofed your dedicated web page, you are ready to select and activate commercial rental web sites for your home.

Your Commercial Rental Sites

Selecting Your Commercial Sites

It is now time for you to select the commercial rental websites that you will use to market your vacation rental home and for you to load these sites with your web input documents. *As soon as your commercial sites are completed, you can expect to begin receiving inquiries on rentals, so this is THE key step in kick starting your rental program.*

In the previous chapter, I summarized my recommended process as 1) selecting some of your rental websites based purely on their web ranking for "hits", or visits and 2) other rental web sites based on your assessment of the competition from other rental properties in your area. I also mentioned that the more sites you contract with, the more inquiries that you are likely to receive. To some extent, the number of websites with which you contract initially is a matter of judgment. I do recommend that you contract with at least five commercial sites initially since the success of your entire rental program depends on occupancy.

Let's consider the most popular sites first. In order to determine this, visit www.alexa.com. When you get to the Alexa home page, walk through the following sequence to get a list of the current top commercial vacation rental sites:

Select "Top Sites"

Select "By Category"

Select "Recreation" as the category

Select Subcategory, then "Travel"

Select Subcategory, then "Lodging"

Select Subcategory, then "Vacation Rentals"

What will be displayed is a ranked list of the most frequently visited sites on the web based on internet visits. At my last review this list included the top 70 sites in the world and showed the top ten (10) sites as:

- Vacation Rentals by Owner (www.vrbo.com)
- HomeAway Vacation Rentals Worldwide (www.HomeAway.com)
- Owners Direct (www.ownersdirect.co.uk)
- Cyber Rentals (www.cyberrentals.com)
- Great Rentals, Inc. (www.greatrentals.com)
- Owners Direct Vacation Rentals (www.ownersdirect.com)
- Beachhouse.com (www.beachhouse.com)
- secondcasa Vacation Rentals (www.secondcasa.com)
- Vacation Rentals 411.com (www.vacationrentals411.com)
- Self Catering Holidays (www.selfcateringbreaks.com)

You may choose to arbitrarily pick from three to five of these websites or spend the time to visit them individually and assess their appeal for yourself. If you elect to take the time to visit them, one way to familiarize yourself with each site is to navigate toward properties in your area that compete with your home. In this manner, you can test the process that potential reenters will go through to view your home, as well as see what the competition is from other properties in your area on these busy and popular sites.

In regards to competition from other similar rental properties in your area, I like to supplement the list of sites chosen based solely on their web rankings by contracting with perhaps slightly less popular sites where the local rental competition for homes like yours is less. In other words, you may find an attractive site that has fewer homes for rent in your resort than other sites, which in turn raises your chance of being selected. When you evaluate competing homes, compare features and prices and amenities to see how you stack up – after all, this is what potential renters are doing! It may sometimes be better to subscribe to a lower ranking website if they have less direct competition from other properties in your immediate vicinity.

Activating Your Commercial Sites

I have found the process of loading personalized rental home data to be very intuitive in most cases, permitting you to cut and paste information from the web input documents which you have previously developed. As you recall, these input documents are:

◊ **General Information**
◊ **Bulleted Highlights**
◊ **Long Description**
◊ **Short Description**

◊ **Home Layout**

◊ **Home Amenities**

◊ **Specific Area Attractions**

◊ **General Area Activities**

◊ **Seasonal Rental Periods, Minimum Stays and Rates**

I suggest that you have these electronic documents as well as your credit card information handy before you begin, then pick a time when you can sit undisturbed for an hour or so to work through the enrollment and loading process. It is not at all difficult since you have already written your marketing information. Now get started!

Availability Calendar and Guestbook

The final step in the online preparation process is to set up an online availability (occupancy) calendar and, if you so choose, a guestbook for your home. You may initiate an online availability calendar at a number of places on the web. Review the Online Resources section of this book for a few suggestions or do your own web research. Whichever provider you choose, you will set up an owner's account which you will use to establish and host your availability calendar.

Setting up an Owner's Account

Your account will provide access to a centralized availability calendar (and at some sites a guestbook) and therefore a central point for data input for multiple commercial sites. When you have successfully set up an account, you will receive a confirming email sent to you from the calendar host advising you that you have successfully registered. You will be given an account, password and calendar ID to use on multiple commercial rental sites.

Availability Calendar

You must get your availability calendar setup before you begin promoting your rental home. The principal advantage of having an online availability calendar is that it establishes a single point of data entry for you at which to enter reservation block outs when they are booked. In other words, you will only need to update one calendar instead of updating a separate calendar for each commercial account – think how time consuming that would be! Likewise, it also provides a central point which may be referenced by all visitors no matter from which commercial rental site their inquiry originates. When properly established and linked by you, your calendar can be automatically accessed by all (or most) of the major commercial rental sites on which you have registered. *Your availability calendar is a critical part of your program and a major time and labor saver!*

You will find that the process for initial setup and activation of your calendar is similar at most calendar providers. 1) Review a few of the free online availability calendar providers and select one, 1) setup and logon to your calendar account, 2) activate the calendar and provide the necessary information to ensure that your initial calendar is up-to-date, 3) record the calendar ID 5) visit each of your selected commercial rental sites in turn and 4) input the calendar ID to the commercial site. Once you have accomplished the initial setup, you will simply log on to your calendar account, go straight to your individual calendar and provide updated information each time you rent or otherwise decide to block out specific dates.

Guestbook

You may also want to establish an online "guestbook". Like the availability calendar, the guestbook can be referenced by many commercial web sites, allowing single point update and eliminating the need for your guests to enter flattering comments about your property multiple times! To get the most out of it, ask your satisfied customers to post favorable comments about their rental experience on your guestbook. What if a guest, however unlikely, decides to enter something not so complimentary? Not to worry – you ultimately control all posted comments.

You will also find that some hosting sites that develop dedicated web pages for vacation rental homes (such as www.vacationhomeadvisors.com of course) will include the initial set up of your availability calendar and guestbook for you. There is nothing wrong with taking a short cut!

Chapter 13

Reservations and Revenue

Effective telephone and email communication and interaction with renters and potential renters will have a major impact on how successful you are in booking rentals for your vacation home or condo. This interaction will present numerous opportunities to display both your personality and your communication skills. Your relationship with your renter begins when you answer a request for reservations. Be prepared to book your guests on terms that work for everyone involved but don't put your financial goals at risk. We will walk you through your options for collecting rents and security deposits, including the use of merchant credit card services. This chapter will help you to understand the fine points of collecting your rental income, important in anybody's book!

- **Taking Rental Reservations**
- **Collecting Rents and Deposits**

Taking Rental Reservations

The first time that you open your inbox and find a rental inquiry will be exciting! In fact, I thought that they were all exciting because inquiries meant money was potentially on the way, but maybe that's just me. If you are prepared, the booking process can be short and sweet. I've handled everything from answering the initial inquiry to sending out the contract package and updating my availability calendar in 30 minutes or less! Just keep a few simple guidelines in mind.

◊ **Be Ready Early**

◊ **Respond Quickly to Inquiries**

◊ **Stick With Your Policies**

◊ **No "Holds" Without Payment**

◊ **Booking Reservations**

Be Ready Early

I never liked to commit to rental rates for the new year until I was finished with the current year. In the interim, I managed my rate changes using discounts or individual negotiations. For my beach rental home, my decision date new annual rates was December 1 since new rate postings needed to be made prior to January 1. For the mountain rental, I was prepared with new rates on or before September 1 since my primary season there was for winter ski vacations. *Shoppers will start perusing the commercial rental sites earlier than you might imagine and you certainly want your postings and web sites to be current, waiting and able to attract and take reservations.* If someone calls based on an old, posted rate that you neglected to update, in my opinion you must honor the old rate if you want any chance to book the rental. And review all of your rates at least annually. Circumstances change from year to year and your competition will be reacting with changes of their own.

Respond Quickly to Inquiries

The single most time sensitive (not time consuming) requirement for self management of your rental property is responding to initial rental inquiries. Individuals looking for rental accommodations are usually inclined to check on several options at the same time, and earlier responders have an advantage. It is an absolute certainty that the majority of rental inquiries have a shelf life of about one day, sometimes less. In other words, if you do not respond to rental inquiries promptly, there is a good chance that the inquiring renter will go elsewhere. After all, the advantages that they count on from using the internet to find their vacation home are the speed and selection that is offered. It is important that you commit to checking and responding to email inquiries as frequently as possible, and that you are able to access your email remotely if you travel frequently. *In my experience, responses sent more than 24 hours after an inquiry is received have a substantially reduced chance for success.*

Stick With Your Policies

Notwithstanding our discussion about having "happy customers", it is just as important to have a happy owner! We discussed the importance of establishing some key rental policies in an earlier chapter. *I encourage you to take the time to thoroughly think through policy issues in the beginning, then to stick with your decisions once they have been made.* You may lose a renter now and again, but you are surely going to gain more attention and approval from those that are looking for what you have. If you decide not to permit pets or you require a financial commitment in order to hold your property, never waiver or compromise. Don't be unreasonable, but you will find that on occasion an apologetic but firm refusal is called for. It is a slippery slope once you begin relaxing your standards. Besides, by sticking to your policies, you won't have to struggle with the same decisions over and over! Of course, one of the beauties of the search feature of commercial rental sites is that you will likely not receive many inquiries from people who can't abide by your posted policies.

No "Holds" Without Payment

I eventually became accustomed to receiving requests for me to "hold" the home for some period of time so the inquiring renter could "check with" somebody before they committed to rent. ***Sorry, but it is foolish for the owner to agree to take the home out of circulation for <u>any</u> length of time without a formal booking – it just blurs the line, confuses the whole issue and opens the door for misunderstanding.*** Explain that you can't hold it, but encourage them to get back to you as soon as possible because you would love them to be your guests! When talking to potential renters, I tried to always be candid about other inquiries that I had received and the risk of waiting, but I never left an open question about who was taking that risk.

Booking Reservations

This is where the whole process comes together. Your documents are ready, you have responded to a potential customer's inquiries and now they have given you a verbal commitment to rent. What do you do next? ***When a verbal deal is reached, simply open your documents folder to access your prepared rental documents and fill out the Guest License Agreement specifically for the renter being booked.*** When complete, save the *Guest License Agreement* as a .PDF file ("print to pdffactory" command) under the individual guest name. Putting the file into a .pdf format reduces the file size for easy email transmission and discourages changes. Save a copy for your records and email a copy of all renter documents to the renter. Ask them to print, sign and return the *Guest License Agreement* by mail with their advance payment, then sit back and wait for a check to arrive!

Collecting Rents and Deposits

I know that you are very excited about making more money on your vacation rental home, but you can't spend it before you collect it! We need to work through the various policies and operational options for collecting rental payments and handling deposits.

◊ **Payment Policy**

◊ **Handling Balky Payers**

◊ **Cancellations and Refunds**

◊ **Trip Cancellation Insurance**

◊ **Merchant Credit Card Status**

◊ **Last Minute Payments**

◊ **Guest Damage and Deposits**

Payment Policy

Establishing a clear and unequivocal payment policy is very important. The following is the language that I used to spell out my payment requirements.

Payment and Refund Policy:

◊ **Reservations made > 30 days out:** All reservations are confirmed with a 50% advance payment due upon booking. Reservations will be canceled if advance payment is not received within seven (7) days of booking; therefore, first or second day expedited delivery is strongly suggested. Balance of rent is due 30 days prior to check-in. **Reservation will be cancelled <u>with no refund</u> if balance of rent is not received <u>at least</u> 30 days prior to check-in.** Reservations must be cancelled within seven (7) days of booking to receive a full refund. Any cancellation occurring after seven (7) days of booking will forfeit the 50% advance payment unless the property is rebooked and confirmed. If the property is rebooked and confirmed, advance payment will be refunded less a $250 cancellation fee. Refunds, if any, will be mailed after the original rental period is complete. Changing a reservation in any way constitutes a cancellation and the same terms apply. There is no refund for inclement or undesirable weather, including hurricane evacuation. **Visit insuremytrip.com for trip interruption insurance and indicate by initialing that you understand this option: _____**

◊ **Reservations made < 30 days out:** If you reserve a time period less than 30 days out, full payment is due immediately by overnight mail and reservations will be canceled if advance payment is not received within five (5) days of booking. If you book within five (5) days of your arrival, payment is due immediately by overnight mail and must be received no later than your day of arrival or reservations will be cancelled.

My language is straightforward, direct and to the point. I cover as many of my exposures as I can think of and try to head off any disputes. This language has gotten me through many successful rentals, but you should feel free to make your own policy. In any case, once you have made a decision, be sure and stick by your policy to avoid confusion and contention.

Handling Balky Payers

What do you do when a renter does not send their payment as agreed, or if a check bounces or you get a chargeback on a credit card? ***The answer is that you immediately put the home back in "for rent" status, while at the same time encouraging the renter to send you their payment so that you can recommit to them for the rental period.*** Here is an example of an email I received from an individual who had committed to rent my home for a prime week. Instead of the advance payment I was expecting, the email that follows was received a week after the reservation commitment had been made.

Good morning Howard! I hope you had a great weekend!

I have good news, okay news and good news. First the okay news - my husband had a little accident in my car last week - no one was hurt but it did take a $1000 bite out of my budget - money I was sending to you. Could you live with $100 as a non-refundable down payment for another week or two? Then for the good news - I will send the whole amount to you at that time. I hate to loose the house for that week and we are really looking forward to coming. If that would be okay - I will get a check in the mail to you TODAY. Also, the other good news - checking the school calendar - I was not aware the kids were going to be out of school Monday, Jan. 9th for a teacher workday. So - the Monday to Monday days will be fine for us - January 2 - 9th.

Please let me know if this arrangement, while not ideal, would work for you to hold those dates for me. If so, I will get that check out to you today. I apologize it took a week to ask you this - was trying to get the damage estimated so I would know what I had to work with. Plastic is expensive!

Have a great day - Pam

Here is my response:

Pam:

I am sorry to hear that you are having difficulties. The home is still available on the night of the second, so staying until the 3rd is not a problem. Unfortunately, I have a hard and fast rule regarding advance payment. As I am sure you realize, now is THE hot time for rental inquiries for the season. I passed on a couple of inquiries just in the last week who were interested in that time period. I can't take a chance with losing that week you had reserved – a prime week – under any circumstances. I am sure you understand that I must re-list the home as available.

I will try to help out some. I will split the total payment into three payments to spread things out a little. If you can send 1/3 today ($567.84), 1/3 to be received by me no later than Nov. 2, and the final payment to be received by me no later than Dec. 2, I can work with that. As soon as I receive your initial payment, I will block the home out if no commitment has been received in the interim. I hope this helps. I have attached a revised lease incorporating the date change you requested.

I hope you can work things out as I would love for you to visit!

Thank you,
Howard R. Jones, Jr.

I received a check for $567.84 almost immediately, and the balance of the rent as stipulated. Note that I incorporated politeness, empathy, an explanation, a recap of the rules and provided an alternative that met MY needs. Importantly, I clearly put the ball in her court to send a check quickly since I specifically say that the home is available for rent until her check is received. And don't forget to send a revised rental agreement!

Cancellations and Refunds

Be certain to spell out your policy for cancellations clearly in your contract. This will deter those few renters who double or triple book different dates with different owners with the intent to cancel based on some "unforeseen" event. I like the idea of fully refunding rent (less a fee) if you are able to rebook. Some fee, perhaps $250, seems reasonable to me in order to deter frivolous bookings and compensate you for some of the wasted time and effort required to go through the booking process. It seems unethical to me to take advantage of someone if you are able to rebook for the rental period, and you are likely to increase goodwill for a future reservation if your cancellation policy is explicit and fair.

Trip Cancellation Insurance

To make it easy for my guests to find and purchase trip cancellation insurance, I like to provide a link to a travel insurance web site in my contract. You will find a couple of representative sites in the section on internet resources. Most of these insurance "brokers" offer insurance plans from a variety of sources, permitting the guest to compare and contrast several options before purchasing. I ask the guest to initial the contract entry as acknowledgment that they understood that they had the option to purchase insurance if they desired. By so doing, the guest is on notice that they are taking responsibility for unanticipated cancellations. In my home state, offering trip cancellation insurance shields the owner from having to make refunds in the event of a mandatory evacuation order if, for instance, a hurricane is breathing down on the rental home. If the trip is cancelled for a covered problem (such as death or illness) the guest is covered not only for lodging costs but also for airfare and other costs. If the guest has declined coverage, they cannot look to the owner to take responsibility.

Merchant Credit Card Status

I mentioned earlier that you should consider applying for merchant status so that you could accept payment by credit card, but that this wasn't absolutely necessary in order to self manage your rental home. Initially, I did not accept credit cards for payment initially for my rentals and, because I required advance payment, I had no problems getting paid. I also had little risk from bounced checks because I also insisted on final rent payment at least 30 days before check in. The major exposure I had was that I required no damage deposit, precisely because I didn't have merchant status and did not feel that I wanted to charge a cash deposit. For any serious damage, I would have had to charge at least $500 and I felt like that much damage deposit would hurt my rentals. However, it is actually a better idea to get merchant status so that you can accept credit cards, at least for damage deposits.

It is also true that many people associate the acceptance of credit cards as a sign of the legitimacy of a business, particularly in light of all the publicity about fraud, so you do get some credibility for your business. There are other good reasons to accept credit cards as well. Some people have credit but not cash and those people will not rent from you unless you accept credit cards. Others are committed to using cards because of reward programs for mileage or points. And even though you pay for the privilege of being a merchant, you will also be getting access to your funds more quickly than if you are waiting on a check to arrive. Your home is also off of the market for up to a week when you wait on a check, while processed credit card charges instantly lock in the reservation.

You may elect to start with a VISA/MasterCard application and add American Express or Discover later if you wish. Programs and fess vary depending on who you apply with so shop around. Most people with average or better credit are easily approved for merchant status. Applications are available at www.paradata.com, www.paygateway.com, www.renters.org, many other websites, or even warehouse clubs like Costco. You will typically process credit card charges directly over the internet by accessing a secure web site using a password and ID. This type of internet data entry is used when the customer is not physically present, such as is the case with email or telephone rental bookings. Costs involved in setting up merchant credit card accounts often include a one-time set-up fee, monthly fees that vary from free to upwards of $500 per year and the discount rate, a percentage of your receipts that the credit card companies charge per transaction, usually in the two to five percent range. Only you can balance the costs associated with accepting cards with the benefits listed above, but my recommendation is to go ahead and apply.

What about the possibility of charge backs? Some owners may be concerned about the possibility of a renter charge back based on some trumped up claim. As long as you have a signed contract that covers cancellation policies and other possible chargeback claims, you should be in a strong position to ultimately ensure collection of funds.

Last Minute Payments

Occasionally, you might receive a reservation inquiry for a period that begins either on the day of inquiry or very shortly thereafter. If you have elected to obtain merchant status for a credit card that the renter holds, last minute reservations present no particular difficulty. However, for owners who elect not to accept credit cards, the standard receipt of a check by mail would not guarantee collection of rent if, for instance, the check does not arrive prior to guest occupancy or is returned unpaid by the bank after your guest has departed. In this case, I suggest that you make arrangements for the renter to deposit cash directly into a bank account. I maintained an account at a large bank with offices located all over the country. I could give the inquiring renter the account number and they could make arrangements to deposit money directly into the account, which I could verify online. This process ensures receipt of payment under all circumstances.

Guest Damage and Deposits

Making repairs is one of the hidden costs of home ownership, and repairs are certainly to be expected when it comes to owning a rental home. I am happy to say that I never had a deposit issue with any of my short term rentals. Maybe I was lucky, but I didn't have merchant credit card status until late in the game, so I did take a chance in the early years. However, my experience was that my guests owned up quickly if anything was damaged and tended to look after my home like it was their own. I believe that one of the advantages from rental self-management is that you have the opportunity to communicate your pride in your home directly to your renters, and to develop some degree of personal connection and relationship with them. When they have the sense that they're your personal guests rather than customers of a faceless property management company, better treatment of your home is the usual result.

Another one of my policies was that I allowed no house parties. I consider house parties to be any group that includes no one over the age of 25. I'm fairly certain that my paranoia was based on the way I acted when I was young! I did everything that I could to discourage house parties, and insisted on contracting with an adult over 25 years old in any group. If you wish to include the college crowd in your target demographic of acceptable renters, I strongly encourage you to obtain merchant credit card status for damage deposit purposes.

A Case for Damage Deposits

Let me explain to you why I am more concerned about damage deposits with long term rentals than with short term rentals. For a couple of years, I sought long term rentals for the off season at my beach house by soliciting renters from the local U.S. Border Patrol training facility and usually things worked out fine. Fine, that is, until one renter decided that my back bedroom would make an excellent kennel for her dog. Since this went undiscovered for the entire term of the six month lease, I found out first hand how much risk there was with long term renters; I had to replace the carpet and paint the entire room! In addition to a damage deposit or credit card, I make certain that any long term rentals that I arrange come with the right of periodic owner walkthroughs.

Chapter 14

Online Owner Resources

Your internet vacation rental experience is made simpler by accessing online information and services, as well as online products and supplies. I'll also introduce my company, VacationHomeAdvisors.com, and discuss the services that we offer. Just like online commercial rental web sites, other online resources can be an invaluable aid to owners trying to maximize the value of their rental property. While I can neither endorse these sites (other than my own of course!) nor pretend that this is an exclusive list, I do think this will be valuable as a starting point for you as you begin to explore the wide variety of internet resources that are available. Some of these sites are for the direct use of owners, while others may be advertised in your promotional materials or provided as an aid to your renters.

◊ **Online Information and Services**
◊ **Online Products and Supplies**
◊ www.VacationHomeAdvisors.com

Online Information and Services

The following section provides categories of different types of information and service resources available on the internet to assist vacation rental home owners in their efforts to rent their homes successfully and to satisfy their renters. It is by NO means an exhaustive list of internet resources, but rather a place to start your search. I encourage you to visit www.VacationHomeAdvisors.com to provide your feedback on your shopping experiences or alternative vendors which you have found to be particularly helpful.

Internet Search Engines

Internet search engines are the gateway to internet content: websites, news stories, images, videos, shopping and more. The rapid rise and use of search engines to find information on the web is a reflection of their usefulness to the general public, and rental home owners are no exception. There are a variety of search engines with slightly different services and tools, so we will just include a very few here. You can find the answer to almost any inquiry, whether it pertains to information, services or products, by just typing in a short phrase if you have internet access.

www.google.com

www.yahoo.com

www.altavista.com

www.momma.com

Free Security Software

As an alternative to paid subscription software, there are numerous products available for free download on the internet to protect your computer. Here are a couple of applications that I have used successfully in the past, but there are many to choose from. You will find many different sites from which the these products may be downloaded.

- AVG Anti-Virus and Anti-Spy Ware Free Option

- Zone Alarm Firewall Free Option

Free Privacy Software

As with security software, there are any number of options for free privacy software available for download, and they too are accessible from lots of different websites. Here are the two with which I am most familiar.

- Spybot Free Option

- AdAware Free Option

Free Rental Listings

Not every place that you advertise your home for rent need be a premium, or fee, service. There are some web sites such as those below that accommodate vacation rental home listing, and don't charge for the privilege. While the use of these free advertising sites is an excellent supplement to your rental marketing efforts, they can't be relied upon as a replacement for commercial rental web sites. However, this is a category that is growing and is limited only by your time and imagination!

www.craigslist.com

www.base.google.com

www.free-rentals.com

Availability Calendars

As mentioned earlier, the use of a single availability calendar to help guests determine whether to contact you with an inquiry is a huge time and effort saver for you. There are several online sources where you may sign up for your own calendar.

www.renters.org

www.getacalendar.com

www.availcheck.com

www.availabilitycalendar.net

Maps and Directions

Whether you choose to include a map for your guests as a part of your introductory package, or prefer to include your street address and information for them to print their own map and directions, the resources available on the web make the process easy. No longer is there any reason for your arriving guests to get lost trying to locate your home!

www.mapquest.com/

www.maps.yahoo.com

www.mapsblast.com

Sales Tax Preparation and Filing Service

We discuss the importance of collecting and remitting taxes that may be required by local and state law in Chapter 15. This responsibility can be made much easier by contracting with an online service. For a nominal fee, these businesses are set up to file returns for your rental home based on your periodic email – simple as that!

www.hotspottax.com

www.avalara.com

www.anybill.com

www.taxcient.com

For Sale by Owner

In Chapter 16, we will discuss several strategies for maximizing your net return from the sale of your vacation home. One of these strategies is to use fixed fee listing services available on the internet to list your home on the local MLS real estate exchange, to provide marketing materials and to guide you through the sales process. A number of these online web businesses exist to help you - I have listed some of the most popular web sites below.

www.forsalebyowner.com

www.homesbyowner.com

www.buyowner.com

www.listbyowneronmls.com

Pet Travel Assistance

Many potential clients include pet friendly accommodations as a key search criterion. If you permit pets, be sure and promote pet friendliness at every opportunity. One accommodation that you may want to make is to include one or more of the following web sites in your introductory letter or in the information that you post in your home.

www.PetTravel.com

www.takeyourpet.com/

www.traveldog.com

www.dmoz.org/Recreation/Pets/Travel/

Language Translation

You never know when you might receive an inquiry from a non-English speaking source, so how do you know what they are saying? There are sites that will translate foreign languages into English, or vice versa. Enter the foreign language text, either in its entirety or reduced to words or phrases, and the automated translator will translate it for you.

www.freetranslation.com

www.babelfish.yahoo.com/tanslate_txt

Income Tax

When I teach any kind of real estate tax class, the one web site that I make certain to mention to my seminar participants is the IRS site. You can find information on most topics relating to your vacation rental home, plus publications that you may order, forms that you will file with your annual return and other tax related material such as an application for an employer identification number if you have employees. Just be sure that you understand that you are getting the official government position, and that there may be another more favorable viewpoint available from your own attorney!

www.IRS.gov

Reduce Junk Mail

Much of the junk mail received in mail boxes throughout the US results from "prescreen lists" sold to businesses everywhere by the major credit reporting agencies. These lists are generated based on criteria specified by the businesses to best reach potential customers, including you. As with unsolicited telephone calls, it is probably in your interest that your rental home mailbox be as uncluttered as possible. As a result of the Fair and Accurate Credit Transactions Act of 2003, consumers have the right to opt out of these mailing lists. In order to do so, simply call toll free 888-567-8688 or visit the web site below.

www.optoutprescreen.com

Silence Annoying Calls

I can assure you that your guests do not want to receive those annoying sales calls while on vacation any more than you would, so take the time and trouble to list your number on this national database. Be sure to remember to revisit this sight if you change your phone number!

www.donotcall.gov/default.aspx

Online Products and Supplies

The following section provides categories of different types of product and supply resources available on the internet to assist vacation rental home owners in their efforts to rent their homes successfully and to satisfy their renters. Like our list of information and services, it is by NO means an exhaustive list of internet resources, but rather a place to start your search. Please visit www.VacationHomeAdvisors.com to provide your feedback on your shopping experiences or alternative vendors which you have found to be helpful. I'll include your information in my next edition!

Rental Home Supplies

As a self manager of your own vacation rental home, you will need regular access to various supplies specifically for rental homes, including such things as specialty soaps, starter shampoos, travel size conditioners and lotions, etc. You may find it convenient to shop locally when you visit your rental home, but you should be aware of several web addresses at which these supplies may be purchased in case you have difficulty finding them otherwise.

www.hotelsupplies-online.com/PPC.htm

www.BathandBodyWorks.com

www.BedBathandBeyond.com

www.aandssuppliers.com

Baby Furniture Rental

Many families elect to travel while their children are young, and this sometimes includes an infant. Rather than tote all the required gear with them, it is often easier and even cheaper for them to rent locally. Providing advance information to your guests about the following web sites may answer questions they have regarding how to handle travel issues associated with small children.

www.babysaway.com/

www.theTravelingBabyco.com

www.thenewparentsguide.com/baby-equipment-rentals.htm

www.travelwithkids.about.com

Trip Cancellation Insurance

You will be doing your renters and yourself a favor if you make the suggestion that they consider purchasing travel interruption insurance for their vacation visit. On the one hand, they may need to cancel for a covered reason and the insurance they purchase may well save them several thousand dollars. In addition, by making the suggestion, you are effectively relieving yourself of the responsibility of dealing with the tricky issue of refunds to renters due to their unfortunate and unforeseen circumstances. In fact, in some states, you may not refuse to accommodate refunds under some circumstances UNLESS you have provided the visitor with information on their option to purchase cancellation insurance to cover their trip.

www.insuremytrip.com/

www.travelproservices.com/rentors.htm

www.travelguard.com

www.tripinsurancestore.com

Locks

Whether for exterior doors or interior closets, the right lock is a key piece of rental management equipment. The two locks that I specifically mentioned in the chapter on home access can be found at the following web addresses.

www.locksmithtoolandsupply.com

www.geindustrial.com

Recreational Equipment Rentals

Generally speaking, you will be well served to use a search engine like Google or Yahoo to find recreational equipment for rent in the local area in which you are vacationing. Very few national internet based clearinghouses exist through which you can arrange for rented equipment to be delivered to your rental home. I suppose that this is because recreational equipment tends to be so regionally specific that it doesn't lend itself to a nation-wide distribution network. I did find one web site that is worth checking out, but I suggest that you tell guests to get on the internet early to make certain that they find what they need locally.

www.rei.com/stores/rentals.html

www.VacationHomeAdvisors.com

VacationHomeAdvisors.com is an internet company specifically created to assist rental home owners in self management of their rental homes. It's my company so please allow me to describe what we do – I think that it's somewhat unique! We offer development and hosting of dedicated web sites for rental homes, free listings of client rental home websites, seminars on rental self management and an online access point to purchase "Making Money on Your Vacation Rental Home" (the book you are reading). There is also an unlisted web site (www.examples.vhallc.com) where you can find a variety of online resources that support rental self management. These resources include online input forms for web site creation and commercial web site population, sample in-home instructions and postings for rental owners, and links to sponsoring and related businesses.

Dedicated Rental Home Web Sites

Our specialty is creating and hosting attractive and functional web sites for the rental homes of our clients. We take you through the setup process quickly and effortlessly so that your vacation rental home is created and ready to showcase your home whenever you are ready to begin renting. Each dedicated web site consists of a home page and multiple subsidiary pages of information and pictures including key links and options as follows:

◊ Home Page with Highlights

◊ Pictures, Pictures, Pictures

◊ Home and Area Descriptions

◊ Rates and Rental Notes

◊ Link to Availability Calendar

◊ Link to Guestbook

◊ A Map to Your Home

◊ Email Contact Functionality

In addition, we include up to five email addresses with each website i.e. yourname1@yourproperty.vhallc.com, etc., although strictly speaking one address is all that is needed to facilitate rental inquiries. The big advantage of using an email address associated with your dedicated web page is that your email addresses are included with your hosting fee, your email address never changes as long as our hosting relationship remains in place and your email address always reflects your home address to remind recipients which property you own.

Seminars on Rental Self Management

I give seminars throughout the country on vacation home self management for owners. Online registration is available for those who wish to attend, along with the dates and locations of seminars. *There is nothing like immediate feedback to reduce uncertainty and facilitate forward progress in renting your vacation home.* In addition, many potential vacation home buyers benefit from getting a clear first hand understanding of what is involved with renting a vacation rental home, what their rental management options are and what even constitutes a good rental home purchase.

"Making Money on Your Vacation Rental Home"

A link to www.lulu.com is provided so that visitors to our web site may purchase the book that you are reading "Making Money on Your Vacation Rental Home". There are discounts for bulk orders for real estate professionals who wish to use the book as a "leave behind" for potential buyers to serve as a primer on the opportunities for self management of a rental home. For some buyers, the additional income available from managing their own rental program instead of relying on a property management company can be the difference in buying a vacation home or not buying, and savvy real estate professionals understand this. It is also a great "thank you" house warming gift for buyer clients to celebrate their purchase and to give them a jump start on the rental process. In any case, book purchases are available in any quantity directly from the publisher in the latest edition and are shipped directly to your specified address.

Vacation Homes for Rent

As a free service for clients, there is also a link to each vacation rental home that we host. In addition to the paid commercial sites on which you list, this is another option for exposure of your home to the renting public. I spend a lot of effort on SEO (Search Engine Optimization – you know, key words and web links) and visitors who understand the importance of renting from dedicated and educated owners can access these rental properties with confidence.

Links to Online Partners

You will also find links to sponsoring websites and some of the online resources mentioned elsewhere in this book, including our favorite commercial rental websites, owner and renter resources, service providers and other online partners.

Available at www.examples.vhallc.com

Why reinvent something that has already been done? On this unlisted but open access webpage, there are numerous samples of web input, renter communication and in-home instructional postings that rental owners want and need. All of these documents may be downloaded, amended and printed for free for your personal rental use.

Web Input Documents - Assemble your information for uploading to commercial web sites and prepare your documents in advance.

Sample Rental Documents – Samples of basic rental documents i.e. lease, directions, home access, etc for you to use as a guide.

Sample Guest Information and Postings - Documents to provide guest information on area activities, home operating instructions and in-home posting.

Chapter 15

Laws and Regulations

Doing a little administrative research in the beginning on laws and regulations will ensure that you are in compliance with all applicable legal and licensing requirements. Be aware of local ordinances which, in some communities, work to thwart the owner manager! We also cover sales and use taxes and have a discussion on several types of insurance that a rental homeowner should consider to protect themselves and their home.

- **Permits and Licenses**
- **Restrictive Local Ordinances**
- **Sales and Use Taxes**
- **Home Insurance**

Permits and Licenses

> *Since laws, licensing, permit and registration requirements for small businesses can vary among jurisdictions, it is critical that you contact your state and local government to determine the specific obligations of your new rental home business.*

.

It is better still, if you are willing to spend the money, to have a local attorney do the research for you to reduce the chance of an oversight. Managing your own rental home generally only triggers requirements for business license and sales tax reporting, but you should be familiar with the various types of federal, state, and local licenses and permits sometimes needed depending on the specific requirements of your locality.

Federal Employer Identification Number

An Employer Identification Number (EIN), also known as a Federal Tax Identification Number, is used to identify a business entity to the federal government. All businesses with employees are required to have one, though keep in mind that independent contractors are not employees. Owners who self manage their own rental homes are not required to have one unless they have employees. You may apply for an EIN on IRS Form SS-4 or directly online at www.IRS.gov as a free service by the IRS.

State Tax Identification Number

Depending on where your rental property is located, your business may also need to acquire a tax identification number from your state's department of revenue or taxation. Each state has its own requirements. We will review the requirements for collecting and remitting sales and use taxes later in this chapter. To assist you in determining what is required in your state, there is a helpful collection of direct links to State government web sites with useful information for businesses at www.IRS.gov.

Fictitious Business Name

If you are doing business as a sole proprietor but calling your business by any name other than your own, you may need to acquire a fictitious business name permit (also called "dba" or "doing business as" permit). These are typically applied for in the locality in which you operate. Most self managing home owners would not be affected by this as they are representing themselves as owners of their rental homes.

Business Licenses/Permits

Many states and localities require a business license for rental home owners in order to legally operate their rental business. This license is typically issue by the local municipality in which your business operates or, alternatively, from the local county if your rental home is outside of the city limits. If you use a property management company, you are probably accustomed to having company personnel coordinate your license application or renewal process. When you move to self management or if you are just starting out, be sure that you understand the license requirements for your community. Contact your local city manager's office or check out the town website for information. While some licenses are fixed fee, it is not uncommon for the license fee to be calculated based on the gross rental receipts from the previous year - the more income, the higher the fee.

Restrictive Local Ordinances

Most localities provide for reasonable business license and other requirements for rental home owners, including absentee owners. *In other localities, however, local laws and ordinances have been enacted which seem specifically designed to curtail, or even eliminate, the use of commercial websites and owner self management.* Ideally, buyers should be made aware of these barriers to rental self management prior to purchasing their rental home, but this is unfortunately not always the case. A description of several types of ordinance requirements, some quite onerous for the vacation rental owner, follows:

◊ **Rental Permit Limitations**: A vacation home rental permit is issued to a specific owner of a dwelling unit. No person shall hold more than one vacation home rental permit. The vacation home rental permit shall be revoked when the permit holder sells or transfers the real property which was rented and the new owner shall apply for and receive a new vacation home rental permit before using the dwelling as a vacation home rental.

◊ **Local Representative:** The property owner shall designate a local representative who permanently resides within the locality boundary or a licensed property management company with a physically staffed office within a given radius of the locality. The owner may be the designated representative only where the owner resides within the locality.

◊ **Guest and Vehicle Register:** The property owner or the designated local representative shall maintain a guest and vehicle register for each tenancy of the vacation home rental. The register shall include the names, home addresses, and phone numbers of the tenants, the vehicle license plate numbers of all vehicles used by the tenants, and the dates of the rental period. The above information must be available for inspection upon request.

◊ **Additional Fees:** The property owner must submit a new local representative form and remit an additional fee if there is a change in the local representative. The locality will notify property owners and/or residents within 200 feet of the vacation home rental dwelling of the name, address and telephone number of the local representative.

◊ **Occupancy Constraints:** The maximum occupancy for a vacation home rental dwelling shall be two persons per bedroom and two additional persons (e.g., a two-bedroom dwelling is permitted a maximum occupancy of six persons). For the purpose of establishing occupancy, a person is defined as an individual as young as two years of age. The maximum occupancy may be further limited by off-street parking requirements. Occupancy of a dwelling shall not exceed twelve persons.

◊ **Parking:** One off-street parking space shall be provided for each three persons of dwelling occupancy. No more vehicles shall be parked on the property than there are designated off-street parking spaces. Inability to provide the required off-street parking will reduce the permitted occupancy. A site plan shall be submitted with an application for a vacation home rental permit which identifies the location of the required off-street parking.

◊ **Solid Waste Collection:** Weekly solid waste collection shall be provided during all months that the dwelling is available for vacation home rental occupancy, regardless of whether or not the home is occupied.

◊ **Permit Posting:** The vacation home rental permit shall be posted within the dwelling adjacent to the front door and contain the following information: (1) the name and telephone number of the local representative; (2) the name and telephone number of the owner; (3) contact information for city hall and the police department; (4) the maximum number of occupants permitted to stay in the dwelling; (5) the maximum number of vehicles allowed to be parked on the property; (6) the number and location of on-site parking spaces; and (7) the solid waste collection day.

◊ **Transient Room Tax:** The property owner must agree to comply with the requirements of the transient room tax ordinance. A room tax is collected from those who rent a vacation home rental dwelling by adding it to the basic rental amount. It is the responsibility of the vacation home rental permit holder to keep an accurate record of the rent and taxes collected. A periodic room tax report will be mailed to vacation home rental permit holders and must be filed with the locality whether or not the house has been rented during that quarter.

◊ **Building Inspection:** The vacation home rental dwelling must be inspected to determine whether it meets the uniform housing code and to establish its maximum occupancy. Uniform housing code requirements cover such items as smoke alarms, adequate escape routes in case of fire, properly operating heating equipment and adequate hot water. Prior to the issuance of a vacation home rental permit, the owner of the dwelling unit shall make all necessary alterations to the dwelling required pursuant to the uniform housing code. An inspection fee of will be charged.

◊ **Building Reinspections:** A reinspection of 20% of the dwellings that have vacation home rental permits will be conducted so that, over a five-year period, all dwellings that have a vacation home rental permit will have been reinspected. A reinspection fee may also be charged. Failure to complete the necessary alterations within 30 days of the inspector's notification of required alterations may result in the revocation of the permit.

Sales and Use Taxes

Most rental owners are obligated to collect sales and use taxes for rental activity and remit these taxes to local and state governments. These taxes go by various names including transient tax, hospitality tax, accommodation tax, lodging tax and so on but it all amounts to the same thing – a percentage of the rent is charged to renters and remitted to the government. Depending on the amount of tax collected, the remittance must be made either quarterly or, when large amounts are involved, monthly. In addition to remitting taxes due, preparation of an accompanying tax return for each government entity is typically required. When an owner uses a property management company, collecting and filing of these taxes is one of the services that is provided, but when a rental home is self managed the responsibility falls to the owner. These taxes generally range from 5% to 15% of rental receipts.

Failure to Comply

Some owners are under the mistaken impression that they can avoid collecting and paying this tax and some even advertise the savings to renters as a competitive advantage over other properties. Wrong! *Failure to remit sales taxes is in many cases a felony punishable by large fines and even jail time.* Let me recant a true story that illustrates how these tax responsibilities are enforced.

Doctoring the Books

A physician in central Florida owned a large and beautiful rental home that generated a lot of income. Since he was managing his own rentals, he decided that it would be an advantage to ignore the collection and remittance of sales tax. For years he used the omission as a competitive advantage in order to maximize his rental income. Eventually, the state authorities discovered this omission and charged the physician owner with tax evasion. As a result, the owner was convicted, paid criminal penalties and fines, lost his home and his professional standing and was incarcerated.

State and local tax authorities administer and audit these tax programs. ***It is a common enforcement practice to identify and prosecute to the maximum a tax violator as a warning and deterrent to other owners.*** It is a big mistake to think that they don't check online renters for tax cheats - it isn't as hard as you think! All they have to do is identify rental homes in their jurisdiction and inquire as to rental costs. If the owner responds that no tax is collected, an audit of rental receipts for past years is undertaken. It is a simple matter to determine whether or not rental income is reported and taxes paid. If you elect to handle reporting yourself, check with your state or local tax office or review the internet information that is available to make certain that you have copies of the appropriate returns stored on your computer for completion and that you understand the legal and timing requirements.

Service Providers

Although the preparation of a sales tax return is typically not complicated, it can be a headache because every taxing authority involved (state, county, city) has their own form and reporting requirements. Add up the time and effort that is involved when dealing with multiple localities and it can require a substantial commitment by the owner. If you prefer to get assistance with preparing and submitting your sales tax returns, any CPA would be glad to help for a fee. A great alternative is to contract with an online tax preparation and remittance service to take over this responsibility. **Web based businesses are available to assist in accumulation and payment of these tax obligations.** The cost is minimal and savings in time and worry can be significant. I have included a couple of online tax filing service web addresses in the Chapter 14 section on Online Services.

Home Insurance

Owners of vacation rental homes have all of the same insurance risks borne by primary residence homeowners, plus other risks specific to absentee landlords. These additional risks include potential liability for guests, increased costs of contents, risky visitor behavior, guest unfamiliarity with home safety measures or simply the inherent risk from the home not being owner occupied. In the insurance world there are a wide variety of coverage options and homeowner requirements and these differ depending on the use of the home. Individual states regulate insurance products on properties within their borders so it is essential to inquire with a local agent in the area in which your rental home is located. Deciding which types of insurance policies are right for you can be a daunting task. Certainly one of the most frightening and financially devastating prospects for a homeowner is losing their home to fire. Fires claim houses every day throughout the country. Many rental homes are in fire prone areas either because they are remote, in windy coastal areas or in hard to access regions, such as on mountain sides. Choosing the right type of insurance to protect you in the event of fire or other risks in your rental home is vital.

Covered Parties

All parties which have an insurable interest in the home should be listed on the policy. Mortgage lenders almost always require that home buyers purchase homeowners insurance as a condition of the loan in order to protect the lender if the home is destroyed. In some cases the mortgagee will waive the need for the mortgagor to carry homeowner's insurance if the value of the land exceeds the amount of the mortgage balance since even the total destruction of the dwelling would not affect the ability of the lender to be able to foreclose and recover the full amount of the loan. The insurance crisis in Florida and other coastal states has meant that some waterfront property owners in that state have had to make the decision to forego insurance on their home due to the high cost of premiums.

Homeowners Insurance

Homeowners insurance, abbreviated in the real estate industry as HOI, is the type of property insurance that covers private homes. It is an insurance policy that combines various personal insurance protections, which can include losses occurring to one's home, its contents, loss of its use (resulting in additional living expenses), loss of personal possessions of the homeowner, as well as liability to third parties who come onto the dwelling and surrounding land. A home insurance policy is usually a term contract - a contract that is in effect for a fixed period of time – and the payment the insured makes to the insurer is called the premium.

The most comprehensive form used for single-family owner occupied homes is a HO3 - All Risk Homeowner Policy. Rather than naming the specific risks covered, these policies provide "all risk" coverage, with some perils excepted such as earthquake and flood. *However, a homeowner's policy generally requires that at least one of the named insured occupies the home. For this reason, if you own a home and rent it out, you may find that many homeowners' insurance policies will not cover damage to your home and will be insufficient to manage your risks.*

Condominium Insurance

Condominium insurance is designed for the owners of condos and includes coverage for the part of the building owned by the insured and for the personal property housed therein. *Condo insurance provides coverage for everything not otherwise covered by the blanket policy written for the entire neighborhood or building.* This additional coverage may even include liability for incidents up to a certain distance from the insured property, all valuables within the home from theft, fire or water damage or other forms of loss. Association bylaws often stipulate the minimum amount of insurance necessary. As with homeowner's insurance, condominium insurance may not cover your risks if you rent your home to others.

Dwelling Insurance

Dwelling insurance, also known variously as fire insurance, landlord insurance, hazard insurance, casualty insurance or property insurance is necessary when the homeowner does not physically live in the dwelling in order to provide coverage from financial losses connected with a property. ***Though not nearly as common as homeowner's policies, dwelling policies are used in some areas of the country to insure seasonal homes that are unoccupied for part of the year, including investment, rental, vacation or seasonally occupied homes***. Strictly speaking, a dwelling policy covers only the structure itself and therefore may provide a much smaller amount of total coverage than a homeowner's policy. When minimal coverage is all that is desired, dwelling insurance is often available at a lower price than traditional homeowner's insurance on the same home.

A dwelling insurance policy itself is a lengthy contract, and names what will and what will not be paid in the case of various events. Many insurers charge a lower premium if it appears less likely the home will be damaged or destroyed as, for example, if the house is situated next to a fire station or if the house is equipped with fire sprinklers and fire alarms. In fact, fire insurance coverage usually requires at least the addition of smoke detectors to qualify for coverage if they are not already in the home.

What Makes Dwelling Insurance Different?

Basic dwelling insurance usually covers damage from fire, collapse, explosion, lightning strike, smoke, vandalism, and wind damage to the dwelling plus any other structures on the property, such as garages or sheds. In addition to coverage of primary physical damage from the above listed exposures, additional coverage at added cost may be available for:

◊ The landlord's personal property used by tenants, such as furniture or appliances.

◊ Rental income when the property is damaged and unavailable for rent.

◊ Alternative accommodation costs for guests who are displaced.

◊ Repairs of accidental damage.

◊ Liability protection for injury to others, including legal defense costs.

◊ Claims due to floods, wind, hail or war.

Optional Coverage

If the above listed optional coverage is desired but not included in the basic policy, it must be purchased separately. *Each insurance policy is different and may or may not include any or all these items so you must discuss your coverage carefully with your agent.* Depending on the particulars of your rental home and personal financial situation, you may specifically wish to consider establishing or increasing the coverage in any of these areas and, in many cases, your lender may require coverage of any of these risks in order to finance your home purchase. Let's look in more detail at a few of the most important types of optional coverage for rental homeowners.

Rental Income Protection

As mentioned above, a possible add-on coverage to dwelling insurance to consider is rental income protection.

> *Depending on your policy, your fire dwelling insurance might pay up to a year's worth of rental value if damage were to occur to your home due to a covered cause and you were left unable to rent it.*

This could prevent you from losing vital income that may be a major part of your financial wellbeing. Since the insurance company pays you what amounts to lost rental income, you are left with time to rebuild or mend your home from the damage and get it back up to par and ready to be rented again.

Liability Protection

Dwelling insurance by itself does not usually include any liability protection for the owner. If you are sued due to a claim of injury from your home or on your home's premises, you will have to defend yourself or be prepared to pay damages to the injured party. **Negligence is often blamed in these cases, but negligence can be a matter of judgment and a homeowner's net worth is at risk without adequate liability insurance coverage.** If your dwelling insurance is secondary to your homeowner's insurance on your primary residence, your existing liability coverage may be extended to cover any incidences in your rental property. Alternatively, some owners elect to purchase an "umbrella" liability policy to protect themselves from risks of this nature regardless of the source of the dispute. If dwelling fire insurance sounds like the best choice for you, keep in mind that there are certain states in the United States that do not make fire dwelling insurance available to its citizens, but allow other options. **Your local insurance agent will guide you as you look into the options available for your vacation rental home in your state.**

Chapter 16

Income Taxes for Rental Owners

In this chapter, we will cover current federal tax law as it relates to the four different ownership tax categories for rental homes and how this classification effects numerous deductions. We will also review tax laws regarding rental income, including the deduction of rental losses against other income, and the implications for and definition of personal use of one's rental property. There are also options to consider when selling rental homes, including an in-depth discussion of my Combined Zero Tax Strategy which may allow elimination or delay of tax when properly applied.

- **Rental Ownership Tax Categories**
- **Taxable Rental Income**
- **Deducting Tax Losses**
- **Personal Use**
- **Ready to Sell?**

Rental Ownership Tax Categories

There are four ownership categories for owners of rental property, each with varying requirements and tax treatments, advantages and disadvantages. As with most important tax decisions, determining which classification is correct for you is a matter of actual individual circumstance, not simply choice. Guidelines and criteria exist to provide assistance on proper tax filing status, but there are some easy to understand definitions that cover the basics. The four categories are:

◊ **Rental Business Owner** - A Business Owner is someone who is actively involved in managing the rental of the home.

◊ **Investor** - An Investor is not actively engaged in the rental process, but seeks to gain from rental income.

◊ **Dealer** - A Dealer buys real estate for the purpose of resale.

◊ **Not-for-Profit Owner** - An owner not engaged in profit making must treat their rental activity as a hobby.

Due to the interest of my readers, we will focus primarily on landlord/owners of vacation rental homes. I am confident that most of you fit into the business owner category since you either own or are considering buying a vacation rental home and are interested in rental self management. But read on to judge for yourself.

Rental Business Owner is the Best!

Filing as a Rental Business Owner provides the most tax advantages for most people. For instance, there are a number of deductions which are allowed for Business Owners exclusively, but not for owners classified as either Investors or Dealers. These are the home office deduction, Section 179 expenses, seminar or convention deductions and start-up expenses. The two key criteria which support business owner tax treatment are 1) a requirement for active owner involvement in management and 2) a demonstrated intent to make a profit. To help make this determination, let's take a look at these two criteria in a little more detail.

Requirement for Owner Involvement

Answer a couple of questions to help determine if you meet the requirements for owner involvement:

Do you work regularly and continuously in the rental process? Business Owners must actively participate in the management of the rental property, either directly or by using property management firms, contractors or other rental industry resources. I have heard it said that using a property management company may undermine Business Owner status for this very reason. Why? Because the property management company usually assumes many of the management responsibilities rather than the owner.

The IRS looks at these situations on a case by case basis since facts and circumstances can vary so dramatically. Owners who use property management firms should take as many opportunities as possible to participate in management and to document that participation. What can you do if you use a management company in order to demonstrate participation? Schedule an annual meeting with your insurance agent to discuss coverage limits. Meet with management company personnel to ask about setting rates for the coming year or to discuss needed improvements to the property. Regular activities such as these will provide a foundation for your claims of active participation.

You can use any reasonable method to document your participation in an activity in a given tax year. You do not necessarily have to keep contemporaneous daily time reports, logs, or similar documents if you can establish your participation in some other way. For example, you can show the services you performed and the approximate number of hours spent by using an appointment book, calendar, or narrative summary.

Copies of emails, records of phone calls and notes from meetings with insurance or property management personnel help to build a case for owner management participation even if a home is professionally managed.

Do you manage more than one property? Managing multiple homes demonstrates regular and continuous involvement in a rental business. Although many people do own more than one vacation rental home, the majority of readers likely own only a single home; thus, this particular criteria is not typically relied upon for landlord filing status.

Is profit your primary motive?

Some rental properties are profitable all the time, year end and year out. Other properties are intermittently profitable, and some even lose money continuously. Evaluating the profit motive perspective involves understanding the range of benefits and motivations that owners have for vacation rental property. For instance, if you allow usage of your home that reflects anything less than a profit motive, you are at risk for losing business owner status. This includes high personal use, including frequent use by family members which we will discuss later.

How does a business owner demonstrate a profit motive?

If you have a rental property that does not continuously generate an annual profit but you have not otherwise disqualified yourself (through excessive personal usage, for instance), there are other tests that may be used to support a presumptive profit motive.

◊ Qualify under the 3 of 5 Test. Beginning with the first profitable year, a taxpayer who achieves a profit in three out of five years is presumed to have a profit motive unless it can be proven otherwise.

◊ Qualify under the Behavior Test. You don't have to actually earn a profit to get the profit motive presumption. Certain behaviors are considered to be evidence of a profit motive. Low amounts of personal and family usage, good recordkeeping, evidence of personal effort, a history of at least some rental income or appreciation, an owner history with other rental businesses, etc. all may be considered when determining if a profit motive exists. *For vacation rental home owners, it is particularly significant that gains in the home's value over time may be considered in the profit motive determination since much of the return on investment in resort rental properties has historically been by way of appreciation.*

Self Management Tax Advantage

Owners who choose to self manage their rental properties are involving themselves more directly and actively into their rental business in a number of ways, often with the objective of increasing income. Therefore, owner self management supports criteria for both owner involvement and the likelihood of making a profit.

> *Assuming the responsibilities of rental self management significantly strengthens the case for tax standing as a business owner/landlord.*

Investor Tax Classification

Investors are owners who do not meet the criteria of being actively engaged in running the business and therefore do not get all of the tax advantages available to the business owner. Rental of property that is only incidental to holding a property for investment is not sufficient to justify more than an Investor classification.

Dealer Tax Classification

Owners of rental real estate who purchase property primarily to resell are classified as Dealers. This category includes speculators, developers, sub dividers, frequent flippers, and real estate converters. This category also includes owners who buy and sell property as part of a business enterprise.

Not-for-Profit Owner

There are very detrimental tax consequences from a rental home being classified as a not-for-profit activity. This treatment may arise from excessive personal use, below market rentals or long periods of vacancy.

Advantages and Disadvantages of Different Tax Classes

Business Owner Advantages

As mentioned, there are number of advantages available to Business Owners exclusively (and not for either Investors or Dealers). These include:

◊ Capital Loss Deductibility. Losses on the sale of rental real estate by Business Owners are fully deductible against all other owner income in the year the loss is incurred under certain circumstances. Investors, on the other hand, are limited in the amount that they may claim as real estate losses on their tax returns.

◊ Maximum Deductions. Much of the advantage of a Business Owner classification comes from the number of deductions allowed against rental income. In fact, all expenses that are considered ordinary and necessary to accomplish rental objectives are deductible. The most common deduction categories are covered in the next chapter.

Tax Advantages Allowed for both Business Owners and Investors (But Not Dealers)

Some tax advantages exist for BOTH business owners and investors, including:

◊ Capital Gains Treatment. Gains on the sale of rental property by Business Owners and Investors are taxed at a lower capital gains rate than that of ordinary income. Dealers on the other hand pay ordinary income rates on gains.

◊ No FICA tax. Rental income is not the same as earned income and thus is not subject to FICA (Social Security) tax. This is a major advantage of rental income over other types of income, notably earned income reported by Dealers in real estate.

◊ Installment Sale Reporting. Both Owners and Investors (but not Dealers) who sell real property over time and collect payment in different years may elect to report income for tax purposes over that extended collection period.

◊ Section 1031 Tax Deferred Exchange. All taxpayers (except Dealers) are permitted to take advantage of tax deferral opportunities available by "exchanging" real estate investment property for "like-kind" investments.

◊ Depreciation Allowed. A big advantage of real estate ownership (again not for Dealers) is the ability to "depreciate" or take a deduction for a portion of the purchase price. This non-cash deduction may be used to offset income, resulting in a tax savings not requiring the outlay of cash.

Not-for-Profit Disadvantages

If a rental home is classified as a not-for-profit enterprise, favorable tax treatment is severely limited:

◊ The only deductions available are those of a second home i.e. interest and tax deductions on Schedule A for an itemizing taxpayer.

◊ All rental income must be reported.

◊ Direct rental expenses may be deducted but only to the extent of rental income and even then only if they meet certain thresholds.

However, gains from the sale of a not-for-profit property that nonetheless qualifies as a second home (but not a third) do normally receive favorable capital gains treatment.

Taxable Rental Income

In the simplest terms, rental income is any payment received for the use or occupation of property. Generally, cash or the fair market value of property you receive for the use of real estate or personal property is taxable to you as rental income. You can usually deduct from rental income the expenses incurred to rent the property, which we will discuss in the next chapter. Income and expenses related to real estate rentals are reported on *Form 1040, Schedule E.*

Cash or Accrual Basis Taxpayer

If you are a cash basis taxpayer, you report rental income on your return for the year you actually or constructively receive it. You are a cash basis taxpayer if you report income in the year you receive it, regardless of when it was earned. You constructively receive income when it is made available to you, for example, by being credited to your bank account. If you are a cash basis taxpayer, you may not deduct uncollected rent because you have not included it in your income.

If you use an accrual method, you generally report income when you earn it, rather than when you receive it. You deduct your expenses when you incur them, rather than when you pay them although there are exceptions for period costs such as insurance. If you are ultimately unable to collect rent that you have previously reported as income, you should be able to deduct it as a business bad debt.

Most individuals operate on a cash basis, which means they count their rental income as income when it is actually or constructively received, and deduct their expenses as they are paid.

Types of Rental Income

Landlords need to be aware of all forms of rental income that are required to be declared. Rental income may include:

◊ Late payment fees.

◊ Charges for guest requested services.

◊ Advance rent payments.

◊ Early termination fees on lease agreements.

◊ Expenses paid by the tenant on behalf of the landlord, although these will likely also be deductible as rental expenses by the landlord.

◊ Fair market value of property or services received in lieu of money.

◊ Lease payments with option to buy. Payments received before the purchase are usually counted as rental income. If the tenant buys the property, payments received after the sale date are generally counted as part of the selling price.

◊ Payments for renting a portion of your home may or may not be taxable income depending on certain thresholds. This would be rare for most owners of vacation homes so we won't go into a lot of detail on this. If this topic is of particular interest, I recommend that you see *IRS Publication 527 Residential Rental Property.*

◊ Security deposits are not counted as income if they are to be refunded at the end of a lease period as per an agreement. Of course, landlords sometimes retain portions of security deposits because tenants don't live up to the terms of a lease - any funds withheld from a deposit are counted as income in the year they are retained. If you keep part or all of the security deposit during any year because the tenant damaged the property or did not live up to the terms of the lease agreement, this money is taxable income in the year this determination is made.

Deducting Tax Losses

Rental properties often generate losses, particularly in the early years when expenses may be higher and a base of return renters has yet to be cultivated. Even when cash receipts catch up to cash expenditures, deductions for non-cash items such as depreciation can still result in a net tax loss. Taking this "passive" loss against other income can result in a significant tax savings. It is important that rental owners understand the laws governing rental tax loss deductibility in order to maximize the benefits and minimize the taxes!

Maximum $25,000 Passive Loss Deduction

Up until about 1978, rental property owners were able to deduct all rental losses regardless of the amount of the deduction, other income or their level of participation in rental management. Congress ultimately determined that this treatment was abusive and the law was changed. The current law is that passive losses generally may only be deducted to the extent of passive income. However, under certain circumstances, owners may deduct up to $25,000 of loss from rental activity from non passive income, such as salary.

In order to qualify for the offset, the rental home owner must:

◊ **Be Within Income Limits**
◊ **Actively Participate in Management**

◊ **Have a Minimum of 10% Ownership**

◊ **Observe Carry Over Rules**

◊ **Special Rules for Real Estate Professionals**

What Income Limits?

Due to the perception that much of the abuse of rental properties in earlier years emanated from owners who had substantial taxable income, limits were placed on deductions depending on the total income of the taxpayer. For taxable incomes up to $100,000, a full deduction up to $25,000 may be allowed. For taxable incomes in excess of $150,000, no loss deduction is permitted. For incomes between $100,000 and $150,000, the loss deduction amount is prorated.

Active Participation Requirements

This "active involvement" requirement is similar to the requirement for establishing a business owner, or "landlord", tax classification. As with establishing a landlord status, owner involvement in management is critical.

Absentee owners who hire real estate management companies to rent their short term vacation rental homes may not be able to pass the active participation requirements for deducting rental losses. Many advisors believe that it is hard to establish that you are actively participating if you live hundreds or certainly thousands of miles from your rental home. If you use a property management company for your home, you should include in your rental management contract that you are the final decision maker on important issues, and keep copies of emails and other correspondence to evidence your involvement in management activities and decision making.

> *Owners who decide to manage their rental properties themselves have a strong argument that they are indeed actively involved in management.*

In addition to other management responsibilities, the direct back and forth communication between the self managing owner and renters to establish dates, rates and scheduling of activities constitutes active participation by any standard.

Minimum Ownership Interest of 10%

Owners are required to be at least 10% owners of the rental property in order to deduct passive losses from rental activity. This effectively eliminates time share owners as these properties are typically divided into smaller ownership groups. Similarly, "fractional" owners may be permitted loss deductibility only to the extent that their ownership interest equals or exceeds 10%.

Carry Over Rules

You may carry any excess loss forward to the following year or years until used, or until deducted in the year you dispose of your entire interest in the activity in a fully taxable transaction.

Special Rules for Real Estate Professionals

There are special advantages to qualifying as a real estate professional when it comes to deducting losses from rental real estate. *In fact, neither the maximum deduction limit nor income limits discussed above apply if you qualify as a real estate professional!* This is a tremendous tax advantage for those who incur large tax losses on rental real estate and who have other taxable income. The requirements are specific, however, and constructed in such a way that more than a real estate license and good attitude are required. Consider the following requirements:

◊ **Real Property Business**: You must be in the real property business of renting your home for profit.

◊ **51% Rule**: You must expend at least 51% of your annual work time in your real property rental business. If you are married, you or your spouse may satisfy this requirement independently of each other.

◊ **750 Hour Rule**: In case you were thinking that 51% of the two weeks you spend working each year is only about eight days, be aware that you (or your spouse if married) must also spend at least 750 hours per year in your real property business in order to qualify.

◊ **Material Participation Rule**: The requirement that you must "materially participate" in the management of your rental home is a higher standard than the "active" participation standard required for limited passive loss deductibility of rental losses by non real estate professionals. If you are married, the material participation of both you and your spouse may be added together to meet the materiality test.

◊ **Not "Employee"**: You may not be an employee of anyone else. If you get a W2 after year end, you are an employee and do not qualify as a real estate professional.

◊ **Direct Involvement**: Direct involvement in rental home management is required. Acting in a professional support capacity (i.e. attorney, accountant, etc.) does not meet the direct involvement criteria.

Personal Use

Among the many reasons that people purchase vacation homes is the opportunity for personal use. It is very important to understand that the amount of time that a vacation rental home is used for personal reasons impacts both the tax treatment of income on a yearly basis and the options for tax planning when the home is sold. Since usage is an area of frequent misunderstanding and often abuse, there are some very specific IRS guidelines for taxpayers who own rental real estate that must be followed in order for the property to be considered a bona fide rental property with full deductibility. It is therefore essential that owners understand these personal use guidelines and document usage activity in such a way as to maximize the deductibility of expenses. The following rules regarding personal use are of critical importance to the owner of vacation rental property.

According to the IRS, if you use a dwelling unit for both rental and personal purposes, you generally must divide your total expenses between the rental use and the personal use based on the number of days used for each purpose. However, you will not be able to deduct your rental expense in excess of your gross rental income. If you itemize your deductions on *Form 1040, Schedule A,* you may still be able to deduct mortgage interest, property taxes, and casualty losses on that schedule even if you do not qualify for full rental deductibility. *If you limit your personal use, the home may still be considered a full time rental home and you may be permitted to deduct rental losses subject to certain constraints and limitations.*

What is the Personal Use Limitation?

Generally speaking, a home may be considered a full time rental home if annual personal use is either under 15 days or 10% of actual rental days, whichever is greater. A day of personal use of a dwelling unit is any day that it is used by:

1. You or any other person who has an interest in it, unless you rent your interest to another owner as his or her main home under a shared equity financing agreement or;

2. A member of your family or of a family of any other person who has an interest in it, unless the family member uses it as his or her main home and pays a fair rental price or;

3. Anyone under an agreement that lets you use some other dwelling unit or;

4. Anyone at less than fair rental price.

As you can see from the above rules, it is generally the case that anytime a vacation rental home is used by an owner or rented for less than fair value rent it is considered personal use. In figuring total personal use time, you must add the time of all owners, so use by any co-owner counts against the total time available for personal use by all owners.

Definition of Family Use

Personal use time in a vacation rental home of course includes the use by the owner or co-owner, but also by any linear family members regardless of the amount of rent charged. Linear family includes children, parents, grandparents, stepbrothers and sisters, step mothers and fathers. Non-linear family includes uncles, aunts, cousins and other relatives. As stated above, the only exception for linear family members is if the home is converted to long term rental for their use as a main home and fair market rent is charged, but in this case the home by definition is no longer a short term vacation rental. Non-linear family who pay fair market rent may use the short term vacation rental home without the time being considered personal owner use.

Repairs and Maintenance

Time spent at the home doing repairs and maintenance does not count as personal use, and travel costs going back and forth to the home are deductible when making repairs or performing maintenance. In order to qualify, an owner or family member must spend the majority of their day (four hours minimum) engaged in work activities. Since this seems to be a pretty good way to avoid excessive personal usage, why not just claim that you are working anytime you visit the home? As good as your word is that you were performing repairs during your visit, it is a good idea to have some proof so that you do not have to rely exclusively on the examiners goodwill if you get audited! My solution was found in the receipts I saved from the local hardware stores. As a rental home owner, if I didn't visit Lowes or Ace Hardware at least once a day, I visited them three times! The receipts I saved for tax deduction purposes reflected key details including date, location and, importantly, a list of things purchased for repair work such as caulk, screens, filters, nails, you name it. This was in my opinion pretty good documentation that I was in town and working on my rental home when I said that I was.

In addition to receipts, I suggest that owners who rely on a property management company to manage their home be certain to indicate that they will be doing repairs and maintenance when they call to block out the home for their visit. Depending on the software in use at their management company, this may be an important record keeping distinction. I have heard stories about the IRS requesting records from property management companies regarding owner block outs and using this information to target abusers. While what is reflected on the company system may not be the final word, it is at least an indication of intent and some documentation that supports rather than contradicts the claims of the taxpayer.

Ready to Sell?

I often recant the Finish saying that a vacation home brings the owner two of the happiest days in his or her life: the day you buy it, and the day you get it sold! Of course, the Finns apparently say this about lots of things, from boats to spouses, but it is true that we go through different stages of life and things do change. Therefore, you may well find yourself moving on and selling your vacation rental home at some point. There are a few unique things that you should consider in regards to tax planning to maximize income and to reduce taxes when selling your vacation rental home.

Primary Residence Exclusion

> *Federal tax laws allow an exclusion from tax for the gain on sale of primary residences up to $250,000 for single taxpayers and $500,000 for married taxpayers.*

The primary criteria for the exclusion are:

◊ Own and occupy the home as your primary residence for a period of time before the sale

◊ Sell the home within three years of leaving

◊ Consider that a partial exclusion may also be available under special circumstances

As is obvious from the title, the primary residence exclusion is NOT available for vacation rental homes. However, this exclusion may be used as a critical component of what I will call the Combined Zero Tax Strategy that can result in no tax owed on the sale of your vacation rental home. We will discuss this strategy shortly.

1031 Tax Deferred Exchange

Often referred to as Section 1031 treatment, this tax law provision permits the owner to sell a rental home and, under strict criteria, replace the rental home by purchasing another real investment property and defer the payment of taxes otherwise due to a later date. A 1031 Tax Deferred Exchange is not a trade, but rather a sale and subsequent purchase. *Current tax law provides for tax deferred treatment for the sale and purchase of any real investment property, including rental homes, as long as the replacement property qualifies as investment property also.* Deferred tax is often just as good as tax free – no tax payment is no tax payment, at least in the short term!

Be certain that you understand the requirements for a 1031 Exchange before you commit to a specific sales strategy, as the requirements cover activities in advance of closing on the sale and are in many ways very specific. For instance, excessive personal use may result in disqualification of the investment property status and therefore will prevent 1031 treatment. Also, a property exchange between two states usually will not qualify for state tax deferral, although the federal tax deferral may be allowed.

Combined Zero Tax Strategy

I often make the statement in my classes that a knowledgeable investor may totally avoid a tax liability on the sale of residential real estate by using my "Combined Zero Tax Strategy". The Combined Zero Tax Strategy combines the tax elimination benefits of the Primary Residence Exclusion with the flexibility of the 1031 Tax Deferred Exchange.

This is not a grey area tax scheme, but rather a tried and true approach that has been used many times in the last ten years by knowledgeable owners and investors. The caveat is that the owner must be willing to 1) take the time required by whichever strategy they choose and 2) adapt their personal living arrangements and lifestyle as necessary to satisfy the requirements of their chosen strategy.

There are several variations on the strategy depending on your objectives:

Example 1: *If you own a residential rental home (investment property), you may choose to stop renting and move into it as your primary residence for at least two years and* **avoid all capital gains tax liability assuming that you are under the adjusted income limits given in the section on the Primary Residence Exclusion above.**

Example 2: *Say you want to retire at the beach and, instead of owning a beach house, you own 100 acres of valuable investment land. If you sell the land outright, you will owe capital gains taxes and have less to invest in your beach house. But you may elect to do a 1031 Tax Deferred Exchange, selling your land and buying a residential rental property observing exchange rules, renting the purchased home out for at least two years, and then moving into the home as your retirement residence.* **No money paid for taxes!**

Example 3: *Now you see where this is going I'm sure! What if you wanted to avoid tax on the sale of your timber land altogether and were not interested in retiring?* **There is no reason that you couldn't exchange the land for a rental house, rent it out**

for two years, move into it as a primary residence, eventually sell it and avoid tax up to the exclusion limits. <u>*You have in effect avoiding paying tax altogether on the investment land that you originally owned!*</u> *In the scenario above, the owner must use the acquired home as a primary residence for <u>five years</u> in order to qualify for the Primary Residence exclusion. Of course, many owners decide that living in a nice beach or mountain house for five years in order to save taxes on a $500,000 gain is not such a bad deal!*

Example 4: *OK, here is the most extreme use of the tax strategy that I can come up with. Let's say that someone has a primary residence of a high value far exceeding the primary residence exclusion – if they sell it outright, they pay a lot of tax. They want to move to another area to live in another high value home and are willing to live somewhere else for four years in the interim. They can choose to (here we go):*

1) *Rent out their primary residence, turning it into an investment property,*

2) *After renting out for two years, exchange it for another rental home,*

3) *Then rent the new home out to others for two years to ensure that it qualifies as investment property,*

4) *Then move into the home as their primary residence,*

5) *Then live in the new home happily ever after (thus paying no tax on the sale of the original home!)*

This last example may be pushing the strategy a bit, but it is a good illustration of the power of combining these two tax laws!

Capital Gains Tax Rates

Capital gains rates are much lower than regular income tax rates for most people, so qualifying for capital gains is a significant tax advantage. ***Taxable gains from the sale of rental homes by landlord owners, from primary residences and from second homes (all owned more than one year) benefit from lower capital gains rates.*** Therefore, even if excessive personal use of your vacation rental results in it being classified as a second home, you will not lose the advantage of lower capital gains rates if you follow the rules.

Sale Timing

We all like to think that we are smart investors and, in your case, I'm certain that it's true! But, based on my experience, I am convinced that luck often plays a part. Vacation and resort markets are typically more volatile in regards to market values than many other real estate markets. Therefore, timing is more important for vacation home purchases and sales than with traditional suburban and urban markets. Of course, we could all be fabulously wealthy if we could time markets like Warren Buffet, but that is seldom the case. So I have no magic formula other than to say that as long as you recognize the potential volatility, are diversified in your investments and stay carefully focused on your own goals, you are likely to time transactions as well as anyone else.

Fixed Fee Listings

If you understand the responsibilities of selling a home and are capable and willing to represent yourself in a sales negotiation, I strongly recommend that you consider using a fixed fee listing service. This is basically a FSBO (For Sale by Owner) process with a huge marketing advantage. For a small fee, you can list your home on the local Multiple Listing Service (MLS) and serve as your own sales agent. In this manner you can eliminate the selling side commission, frequently in the range of 3% of the sales price. A buyer agent commission (often in the same 3% range) must still be paid in order to list on MLS and to encourage agents to inform their interested buyers, but cutting your total commission in half can be a tremendous savings.

You will have to reside close to the property being sold in order to show your home on short notice. For this reason, owner selling might not work for many absentee owners. You will make home showing appointments, comply with legal requirements and ultimately understand and approve the sales contract. Some of the most popular web based fixed fee web sites are listed in the previous chapter on internet resources.

Rental Income History

Savvy buyers and sellers of rental real estate expect to include a rental income history as a part of the sales negotiation. Smart buyers insist on seeing documentation of rental income, not just assurances and promises. Smart sellers understand that a strong rental history helps make the case for a good rental property and a premium sales price.

In either case, be certain that the rental income documentation accounts for all gaps in rentals, be they personal use, downtime for repairs, etc. Some buyers will ask for a copy of your tax return, or at least of your *Schedule E Rents and Royalties*, but this is something that I wouldn't provide simply because of privacy concerns regarding my tax return. Instead, you might offer your own schedule broken out for different time periods and different rates. You should expect to provide support for your schedule in the way of contracts or specifics. For owners who use a property management company, a printout is usually available which details income and expenses processed through their system. A buyer would be foolish to accept as adequate documentation an unsubstantiated schedule with verbal assurances that it is "absolutely correct".

Chapter 17

Landlord Expense Deductions

If we assume that you qualify for renal business owner status due to your circumstances and want to save money on taxes, you should have a basic understanding of the types of and requirements for operating expenses that you may deduct from rental home income. We will start with a look at the overall requirements for deducting operating expenses, examine a number of commonly encountered rental home operating expenses, review the basics of the home office deduction requirement and computation, and address the tax implications for any hiring decisions that an owner makes. We will also take a look at several special tax situations which may be available to the rental homeowner.

- **A Basic Understanding**
- **Expense Deductions**
- **Operating Expenses**
- **Home Office Deduction**
- **Hired Help**
- **Special Tax Situations**

A Basic Understanding

I hope that you are not intimidated by the mention of "taxes" as some people seem to be. I assure you that I will present you with just the basics. **Your CPA, accountant or attorney can help you when it comes to making any decisions on the exact amount and nature of your deductions, but in the meantime you can get a good understanding with just a little effort.** Having a personal and direct understanding of rental deductions is important since you are the one making the decisions, paying the bills and keeping the records!

Most of the typical costs that you pay which are associated with your rental home are deductible, including utilities, cleaning, insurance, and others. There are other expenses that are restricted in some way, either in amount or by the nature and extent of documentation required. In addition, there are a few specifically excluded deductions of which you should be aware.

Expense Deductions

Taxpayers who qualify for the advantageous tax treatment of landlord/rental business owners must file *Schedule E Rents and Royalties* with their tax return to document taxable rental activity and to report rental income. To offset taxable rental income, the taxpayer is allowed to deduct the expenses associated with operating the rental "business". *In many cases where a mortgage exists on the property, the combination of mortgage interest, depreciation and operating expenses will result in no net income, and even a net loss.* This net loss may be used to reduce other non rental income in some cases as discussed in the previous chapter, providing the owner with tax savings to offset the rental loss. In order to deduct operating expenses of operating your rental business, the expenses must meet several general criteria, plus a couple of specific ones:

◊ **Ordinary and Necessary**

◊ **Applicable to the Current Period Only**

◊ **Directly Related to the Rental Activity**

◊ **Reasonable**

◊ **Not Prohibited**

Ordinary and Necessary

The expense should be one that is both ordinary and necessary in the normal course of business in order to operate your rental program. Since no comprehensive list of allowed expenses is provided by the IRS, judgment is required as it is in many areas of tax law compliance. However, the IRS typically does not challenge operating expenses unless they are clearly frivolous or unrelated to the rental activity. It is hard to imagine a direct expense for a rental home that would be challenged as frivolous or unnecessary since the owner is trying to appeal to as diverse a group of potential renters as possible. I suppose an example of a frivolous charge might be a deduction related to throwing a party "for potential renters" or other self serving costs.

Applicable to the Current Period Only

Operating expenses must be related to the period of time that the tax return covers. Since most rental business owners of single family vacation rentals are cash filers, they file on a calendar year basis. If a rental expense covers a period beyond the current tax calendar year, the expense deduction must be prorated appropriately. Likewise, no deduction is permitted for uncollected rents since presumably no income was ever recognized.

Directly Related to the Rental Activity

Deductions are allowed for things that increase rent, improve renter experience, are required for home maintenance, or other expenditures that support the rental effort. Expenses incurred for items or services that do not relate to the management of the rental activity may not be deducted. This would include such things as personal toiletries, home supplies that are not available for guests, services which cannot be accessed by rental guests (i.e. internet restricted to owner use), local purchases made for non-home related items (golf fees, dry cleaning, etc.).

Reasonable

Only expense amounts that are for items or services that are reasonable in quantity, amount or application may be deducted in a given year. It is clearly reasonable to pay for some administrative assistance to keep track of things, but I suggest that it would <u>not be</u> reasonable to pay your 10 year old daughter $10,000 during a tax year to help with the books! Likewise, spending $50 to purchase beach toys and balls for a beach rental home would be understandable, but it would likely be questioned if you deducted $2,500 spent during the year on local jet skis and bike rentals.

Not Prohibited Deductions

Certain types of expenditures by rule may not be deducted as rental expenses. These often include expenses which would otherwise qualify under the "ordinary, necessary and reasonable" requirements, but are specifically excluded as deductions by law. The non deductible expenses include government penalties, fines and tickets, federal income taxes paid, political contributions, and expenses that exceed specific threshold amounts as we will discuss on the following pages. In addition, keep in mind that some expenses which are not deductible on Schedule E may be deducted elsewhere i.e.

charitable contributions are only deductible by individuals on *Form 1040, Schedule A.*

Now let's consider several brainteasers that highlight the finer points of deductibility.

Rental Donation Brainteaser

Let's briefly consider the situation where a vacation rental owner decides to donate a week of prime rental season in a beach front rental home to the local telethon for charity. And let's say that this donated week normally and regularly rents for $3000 during this time of year. My question: is the owner entitled to a deduction on his Schedule E for the foregone rent? The answer is no. To take a deduction for rent neither recognized nor received would amount to a double deduction. Consider that the owner will get all the deductions to which he or she is normally entitled such as utilities, cleaning, interest, etc. because these are expenses that were paid and which covered the term of the rental. If a separate deduction was going to be taken for foregone rent, the owner would need to recognize this rent as income, with the result being a wash out of the two and no different from not deducting the foregone rent at all!

Repair Time Brainteaser

A similar issue with a similar answer has to do with the deductibility of an owner's labor when it is contributed to the repair or upkeep of the rental home. As the owner of a vacation rental home, there are many occasions when you may purchase materials and spend time repairing damage to your home such as interior painting. The purchased materials are obviously deductible, but what about the value of your time spent? As above, there is no deduction allowed for any "imputed" cost of labor as this would require reporting the amount as income which would offset the deduction exactly. The benefit to the owner is in the cost savings and the presumed increased value of the properly maintained home.

Capital Improvement Brainteaser

Finally, suppose you as the owner decide to build an addition onto your home, let's say a carport, and you are going to do the work yourself. It is clear that any materials or other out of pocket costs you incur for the job are eligible as additions to the homes basis, thus decreasing the taxable profit realized when the home is sold. Can you also add an amount to your home's basis for your valuable time and effort? Sorry, but the answer is no. No cash money was spent to pay you for your time. Your benefit is the cash that you saved by doing the work yourself and the financial benefit of your effort will presumably be realized when the home is sold.

Operating Expenses

IRS Schedule E Rents and Royalties lists broad categories of operating expenses that reflect the typical mix of costs involved in rental home ownership, but an expense category does not have to be listed to be deductible. **As you read the information on expenses that I have provided below, I hope that you will conclude that federal tax laws generally are reasonable and appropriate and, usually, not too difficult to understand.** You may deduct your ordinary and necessary expenses for managing, conserving, or maintaining rental property from the time you make it available for rent. Keep in mind that the most difficult issues in tax law are always the ones that are on the margin, somewhere between deductible and not deductible. We accountants call these the "grey areas" and are one reason that you should have a CPA help you. I'm not interested in educating you to be a tax accountant. (I'm confident that you wouldn't want me to even if I could!) So let's take a look at the following expense categories from the point of view of the rental business owner:

Management Commissions

Many readers have decided to self manage their rental homes and will therefore not be concerned with management commissions since they don't pay them. For other owners who do rely on the services of property management companies, payment for management commissions is a regular and sizeable deduction.

Car and Travel Expenses

If you use your car to travel to your rental home in order to "actively manage" your rental, you may deduct the cost for both travel to and from the home and for local mileage. This includes meetings with local property managers, service providers or your insurance agent. You must properly allocate your expenses between rental and non rental activities and you cannot deduct the cost of traveling away from home if the primary purpose of the trip is not to improve the property. Typically, for vacation rental home owners, the standard mileage deduction is the preferred method. Please visit www.irs.gov and refer to *IRS Publication 463 Travel, Entertainment, Gift and Car Expenses* for the current standard mileage rate. This rate can change frequently and is often different for different periods of the year due to rapidly changing fuel costs. If you use the standard mileage rate, you can add to your deduction any parking fees and tolls incurred for business purposes, but not specific charges to maintain or repair your vehicle.

Insurance (Fire, Theft, Flood, Liability)

You may deduct the cost of insurance paid for rental property coverage. If you pay an insurance premium for more than one year in advance, you can deduct only the part of the premium payment that will apply to the current tax year. You cannot deduct the total premium in the year you pay it even if you are a cash basis taxpayer.

Taxes (Real and Employment)

Real estate taxes are deductible for federal tax purposes as long as they are ad valerum taxes, or taxes which are computed based on the home's value. Along with interest expense, these deductions may be taken as rental expenses or, alternatively, as a personal deduction on *IRS Schedule* A if excessive personal use precludes treatment of your home as a rental business. Employment taxes will be paid only if an employee is hired - see the discussion on this topic later in this chapter.

Advertising

Payments for commercial web sites are the most common advertising expense incurred by self managing rental property owners. Very rarely are additional payments for magazine, newspaper or other advertising expenses necessary. If you decide to print business cards or brochures to leave in the home, these expenses would be categorized as advertising.

Cleaning

Payments for housekeeping service can be expected to vary proportionally with rental income. In addition, annual cleanings, window cleanings and occasional expenditures for exterior washings of decks and porches can be expected and are deductible.

Utilities

Unlike with long term rentals, utilities like electricity, gas and water are included in the price for short term rentals and therefore contribute significantly to the cost of maintaining a rental home. This is one of the biggest differences between short term vacation rentals and long term rentals, and a reason that owners are able to enjoy personal use of their vacation rental properties. Utility deposits are not a deductible expense since they are expected to be eventually refunded.

Repairs, Improvements and Depreciation

You can deduct the cost of repairs to your rental property, but you cannot deduct the cost of improvements. The cost of improvements is recovered by taking depreciation.

Depreciation - You can begin to depreciate rental property when it is ready and available for rent. Depreciation of rental property is a complex issue and should be dealt with in consultation with your accountant or other tax preparer.

Repairs - A repair keeps your property in good operating condition. It does not materially add to the value of your property or substantially prolong its life. Repainting your property inside or out, fixing gutters or floors, fixing leaks, plastering, and replacing broken windows are examples of repairs. However, if you make repairs as part of an extensive remodeling or restoration of your property, the job as a whole may be considered to be an improvement.

Improvements - An improvement adds to the value of property, prolongs its useful life, or adapts it to new uses. If you make an improvement to property, the cost of the improvement must be capitalized. The capitalized cost can generally be depreciated as if the improvement was a separate property and it is often advantageous to do so. The following have been identified as examples of improvements by the IRS:

Examples of Capital Improvements

Additions

Bedroom

Bathroom

Deck

Garage

Porch

Patio

Miscellaneous

Storm windows, doors

New roof

Central vacuum

Wiring upgrades

Satellite dish

Security system

Plumbing

Septic system

Water heater

Soft water system

Filtration system

Lawn & Grounds

Landscaping

Driveway

Walkway

Fence

Retaining wall

Sprinkler system

Swimming pool

Heating & Air Conditioning

Heating system

Central air conditioning

Furnace

Duct work

Central humidifier

Filtration system

Interior Improvements

Built-in appliances

Kitchen modernization

Flooring

Wall-to-wall carpeting

Insulation

Attic

Walls, floor

Pipes, duct work

Schedule courtesy of the IRS

Loan Expenses

Some loan expenses may be deductible immediately, some over time and others not at all.

Interest - You may deduct mortgage interest you pay on your rental property. If you paid $600 or more of mortgage interest on your rental property to any one person, you should receive a *Form 1098, Mortgage Interest Statement*, or similar statement showing the interest you paid for the year. Chapter 4 of *IRS Publication 535* explains mortgage interest in detail.

Points - The term "points" is often used to describe some of the charges paid, or treated as paid, by a borrower to take out a loan or a mortgage. These charges are also called loan origination fees, maximum loan charges, or premium charges. Any of these charges (points) that are solely for the use of money are interest. Because points are prepaid interest, you generally cannot deduct the full amount in the year paid, but must deduct the interest over the term of the loan. The exception is for points paid on the first financing of a primary residence. Points paid for financing of rental investment property may not be deducted in full when paid but instead may be amortized (deducted) over the life of the loan. If your loan or mortgage ends short of full term, you may be able to deduct any remaining points in the tax year in which the loan or mortgage ends. A loan or mortgage may end due to a refinancing, prepayment, foreclosure, or similar event. However, if the refinancing is with the same lender, the remaining points generally are not deductible in the year in which the refinancing occurs, but may be deductible over the term of the new mortgage or loan.

Mortgage Fees - Certain expenses you pay to obtain a mortgage on your rental property cannot be deducted as interest. These expenses, which include mortgage commissions, abstract fees, and recording fees, are considered capital expenses and must be amortized over the life of the mortgage. See *IRS Publication 535* for information about amortization.

Legal and Accounting

Owners must be careful to segregate business and personal expenses. You can deduct, as a rental expense, the part of tax return preparation fees you paid to prepare *IRS Schedule E, Part I.* For example, on your 2008 *Schedule E* you can deduct fees paid in 2008 to prepare Part I of your 2007 *Schedule E.* You can also deduct, as a rental expense, any expense (other than federal taxes and penalties) you paid to resolve a tax underpayment related to your rental activities.

Local Benefit Taxes and Special Homeowner Assessments

Generally, you cannot deduct charges for special assessments and local benefit taxes that increase the value of your property, such as charges for major improvements, putting in streets, sidewalks, or water and sewer systems. These charges are non depreciable capital expenditures, and must be added to the basis of your property. However, you can deduct assessments and local benefit taxes that are for maintaining or repairing the above listed improvements.

Vacant Rental Property

If you hold property for rental purposes, you may be able to deduct your ordinary and necessary expenses (including depreciation) for managing, conserving, or maintaining the property while the property is vacant. However, you cannot deduct any loss of rental income for the period the property is vacant. If you sell property you held for rental purposes, you can deduct the ordinary and necessary expenses for managing, conserving, or maintaining the property until it is sold.

Home Office Deduction

Generally, expenses related to the rent, purchase, maintenance and repair of a personal residence are not deductible. ***However, if you are classified as a business owner/landlord of your rental property, you may be entitled to take a deduction for the expenses of maintaining an office in your home if you use part of your home for business purposes.*** This deduction can represent a substantial tax savings opportunity.

In order to claim a business deduction, you must file *IRS Form 8829 Expenses for Business Use of Your Home* and use part of your home in <u>at least one</u> of the following capacities:

◊ As the principal place of business where you exclusively and regularly perform management or administrative duties related to your rental home, or

◊ As a regular place to meet or deal with customers or suppliers in the normal course of your rental business, or

◊ For regular storage of supplies, records, furniture, inventory or equipment related to your rental home.

Exclusive Use

You may only deduct the expenses of a separate area or structure at your home if it is used regularly and exclusively for your rental business. "Exclusive use" means that the area of the home designated as your home office is used only for trade or business and may not be used for any other purpose. "Regular use" means the area is used regularly for trade or business - incidental or occasional business use is not regular use.

What Calculation Methods are permitted?

Generally, the amount of the deduction depends on the percentage of the home that is used for business. The home office deduction calculation starts with determining this business usage factor specific to your individual circumstances. A taxpayer can use any reasonable method to compute the business usage factor depending on what results in the most favorable outcome, but the most common methods are:

◊ Percent of Total Square Feet - Divide the area of the home used for business by the total area of the home, or

◊ Number of Rooms - Divide the number of rooms used for business by the total number of rooms in the home if all rooms in the home are about the same size.

The area does not have to be a "room" as long as it is an area used exclusively as per the previous discussion. No separate entrance or special business "zoning", etc. is required as long as IRS requirements are met.

What Expenses Could I Deduct?

The list of costs that may be considered for a home office deduction is long. In order to be considered, these costs must be related to regular and exclusive business use that can be clearly distinguished from personal use or reasonably allocated between the two. When figuring your home office deduction, consider the following costs:

◊ **Rent** (Prorated) - If you rent the home you occupy and meet the requirements for business use of the home, you can deduct part of the rent you pay. To figure your deduction, multiply your rent payments by the percentage of your home used for business.

◊ **Homeowners Insurance** (Prorated) - You can deduct the cost of insurance that covers the business part of your home. However, if your insurance premium gives you coverage for a period that extends past the end of your tax year, you can deduct only the business percentage of the part of the premium that gives you coverage for your tax year. You can deduct the business percentage of the part that applies to the following year in that year.

◊ **Association Dues** (Prorated) - If you are required to pay dues to a neighborhood association as a requirement for owning your home, a portion of these charges may be included as a business expense.

◊ **Repairs and Maintenance** (Direct or prorated) - The cost of repairs that relate to your business, including labor (other than your own labor), is a deductible expense. Repairs keep your home in good working order over its useful life. Examples of common repairs are patching walls and floors, painting, wallpapering, repairing roofs and gutters, and mending leaks.

◊ **Housekeeping** (Direct or prorated) - If you employ a housekeeper to maintain your home and the duties include cleaning of your home office, you may deduct a prorated portion of the cost as a business expense.

◊ **Utilities** (Prorated) - You can deduct the business part of expenses for utilities and services, such as electricity, gas, trash removal, and cleaning services. Generally, the business percentage for utilities is the same as the percentage of your home used for business.

◊ **Security System** (Prorated) - If you install a security system that protects all the doors and windows in your home, you can deduct the business portion of the expenses you incur to maintain and monitor the system. You also can take a depreciation deduction for the part of the cost of the security system relating to the business use of your home.

◊ **Pest Control** (Prorated) - If you require a pest service to keep your home free from bugs, you may deduct a portion of the monthly cost as a business expense.

◊ **Depreciation** - If you own your home and qualify to deduct expenses for its business use, you can claim a deduction for depreciation. Depreciation is an allowance for the wear and tear on the part of your home used for business. Remember that you cannot depreciate the cost or value of the land.

◊ **Telephone** - Telephone service charges, including taxes, for the first phone line into a home is a nondeductible personal expense. However, charges for business long-distance phone calls on that line, and the cost of a second line used exclusively for business, are deductible business expenses.

Mortgage Interest and Property Taxes

Mortgage interest and real estate taxes may also be deducted in a prorated fashion as an expense relating to the business use of your home. Whenever I make this point in class, it is generally acknowledged, but with the frequent observation by someone that these expenses are already deductible as an itemized deduction on *Schedule A* for taxpayers who choose to itemize. But consider the tax savings available by transferring the portion of interest and taxes that relate to business use to your *Schedule E*. Since income from rental activity is not subject to social security related taxes (FICA and Medicare), an additional savings of approximately 15.3% on taxes is available from deductions which are shifted from *Schedule A* to *Schedule E*!

Deduction Limit

If your gross income from the business use of your home equals or exceeds your total business expenses (including depreciation), you can deduct all your business expenses related to the use of your home. However, if your gross income from the business use of your home is less than your total business expenses, your deduction for certain expenses for the business use of your home is limited.

Your deduction of otherwise nondeductible expenses such as insurance, utilities, and depreciation (with depreciation taken last) that are allocable to the business is limited to the gross income from the business use of your home minus the sum of the following:

◊ The business part of expenses you could deduct even if you did not use your home for business (such as mortgage interest, real estate taxes, and casualty and theft losses that are allowable as itemized deductions on *Schedule A* plus

◊ The business expenses that relate to the business activity in the home (for example, business phone, supplies, and depreciation on equipment), but not to the use of the home itself.

If your deductions are greater than the current year's limit, you can carry over the excess to the next year. If deductions are carried over to the year in which the home is sold, the carried over deductions may be used to increase the basis of the home and, therefore, lower any capital gains taxes due.

Recordkeeping for a Home Office Deduction

The following are suggestions for documenting your home office deduction but are not specifically required by the IRS.

- Keep copies of all expense documentation and worksheets used in your home office calculations.

- Take a picture of your home office and draw a diagram showing your home office as it relates to the home as a whole.

- Send all rental business related mail to your home.

- Be sure and use your home address on all your business cards, stationary and business filings.

- Use a separate telephone line for your business and keep that phone in your home office.

- Maintain a log, journal or calendar listing your home office activities.

Other Limitations

The following are some of the most commonly considered limitations when it comes to taking the home office deduction:

◊ Non-business profit-seeking endeavors such as investment activities do not qualify for a home office deduction, nor do not-for-profit activities such as hobbies.

◊ Taxpayers may not deduct expenses for any portion of the year during which there was no business use of the home.

◊ If the use of the home office is merely appropriate and helpful but not necessary, you cannot deduct expenses for the business use of your home.

The requirements for Home Office Deductions are discussed in greater detail in *IRS Publication 587, Business Use of Your Home.*

Hired Help

Keep in mind that our discussion covers only federal tax laws. Depending on where your vacation rental home is located, where you live or where you file your returns, state laws may affect your tax planning and calculations. As always, before you make any irrevocable decision, consult your tax advisor.

Family Members

One of the advantages of operating your own business is hiring family members, and there is no law that says that you may not employ family members to assist in managing your rental home. If you are a self-manager, there are certainly more opportunities to justify this than if you rely on the services of a property management company, since you must of necessity perform certain clerical, email and other duties that are not required otherwise. The key criteria involve the reasonableness of both the required duties and the amount of pay. In other words, you must be sure that the duties performed are reasonable given the age, education and maturity of the family member in order to justify the employee relationship and associated wages.

Child Employed by Parents

The tax advantages of employing a family member extend principally to employing your child since they may exempt nominal amounts of income from tax, and incur a tax burden less than your own on higher amounts. Qualifying child employees only pay federal income tax on wages in excess of the standard deduction, which was $5700 in 2009, so zero tax is due on amounts lower than this threshold. In addition, given the progressive nature of the tax rates at lower income levels, you may benefit from shifting income to your child. For instance, your child would have to pay only 10% on taxable income in 2009 up to $8350. Since taxable income is total income minus the aforementioned standard deduction, your child employee could earn as much as $14, 050 and never pay a rate higher than 10% on any of it. If your children are likely to incur expenses of their own which can be paid for with tax advantaged income, it may be worth satisfying the requirements to employ your offspring. Be aware that, like all other employees, payments for the services of a child are subject to income tax <u>withholding</u> regardless of age if the total income earned in the year is expected to generate a federal income tax liability.

In addition to federal income tax savings, there are other tax advantages. Payments for the services of a child under age 18 who works for his or her parent in a trade or business are not subject to FICA (social security), Medicare or Federal Unemployment Tax Act (FUTA) taxes if the trade or business is a sole proprietorship, or a partnership in which each partner is a parent of the child. Payments for the services of a child between the age of 18 and 21 who works for his or her parent in a trade or business are not subject to FUTA but are subject to social security and Medicare taxes. Keep in mind that wages for the services of a child <u>are</u> subject to social security, Medicare, and FUTA taxes if he or she works for:

◊ A corporation, even if it is controlled by the child's parent,

◊ A partnership, even if the child's parent is a partner, unless each partner is a parent of the child, or

◊ An estate, even if it is the estate of a deceased parent.

Spouse Employed by Taxpayer

Although the income shifting advantages of employing your child in your business do not extend to your spouse, there may be other reasons that it makes sense. For instance, you may be able to provide health or accident insurance to your spouse as an employee which would not otherwise be available as a non-employee. Another benefit is that the cost of deducting travel for business purposes would include the spouse's expenses if his or her presence is related to the business.

Independent Contractor versus Employee

While hiring of a housekeeper is the most common personnel decision that a landlord has to make, there are other occasions in which knowledge of employment laws and regulations also may have a bearing, such as when arranging maintenance, repair, clerical and others duties. Unless you arranging for the employment of a family member as outlines above, steps should be taken to ensure that you do not enter into an employer to employee relationship instead of that of an independent contractor. An employer to employee relationship entails financial, tax and reporting responsibilities and is generally not necessary or advised in managing a rental home.

According to the IRS, in order to determine whether a worker is an independent contractor or an employee under common law, you must examine the relationship between the worker and the business. All evidence of control and independence in this relationship should be considered. The facts that provide this evidence fall into three categories - behavioral control, financial control, and the type of relationship itself.

Behavioral Control - This covers facts that show whether the business has a right to direct or control how the work is done through instructions, training, or other means. When hiring a housekeeper, for instance, a landlord may require a high quality outcome, but they should leave the method and approach to achieving this outcome to the individual hired.

Financial Control - This covers facts that show whether the business has a right to direct or control the financial and business aspects of the worker's job. This includes:

◊ The extent to which the worker has unreimbursed business expenses. For instance, the landlord should require that the housekeeper provide their own cleaning supplies and compensate them accordingly.

◊ The extent of the worker's investment in the facilities used in performing services. For instance, the landlord should not generally provide common cleaning tools but instead request that the housekeeper provide their own.

◊ The extent to which the worker makes his or her services available to the relevant market. It is advantageous that the housekeeper has or attempts to have other clients in the local market.

◊ How the business pays the worker, and

◊ The extent to which the worker can realize a profit or incur a loss.

The payment for services should be and generally is fixed fee in order to avoid problems with these last two requirements.

Type of Relationship - This covers the facts that show how the parties perceive their relationship. This includes:

◊ Written contracts describing the relationship the parties intended to create. A simple agreement that refers to an independent contractor relationship and incorporates suggestions in this paragraph is helpful.

◊ The extent to which the worker is available to perform services for other similar businesses. As above, the fact that your contractor does similar work for other clients is supportive of an independent contractor relationship.

◊ Whether the business provides the worker with employee–type benefits, such as insurance, a pension plan, vacation pay, or sick pay. Offering ancillary payments, benefits or compensation may support a finding of an employer to employee relationship.

◊ The permanency of the relationship. Any contract terms should be established based on a fixed term, such as a year, with termination at will and renewal provisions included as necessary.

◊ The extent to which services performed by the worker are a key aspect of the regular business of the company. Certainly cleaning of the rental home is regular and continuous so some effort should be made to follow the above guidelines to avoid problems with the IRS.

> *The above detailed rules notwithstanding, the employment of an individual or company to clean your vacation property is seldom the type of relationship that meets the definition of employee.*

It is important to know the rules in order to avoid the "employee" classification. While a determination may be obtained proactively directly from the IRS on a specific relationship, this is generally not necessary if proper steps are taken to properly define the parameters of the job.

Filing 1099s

Keep in mind that landlords, like other business owners, are required to file Form 1099s with the IRS in February for the past year for any contractor to which more than $600 is paid annually. 1099 filing requires obtaining of a social security or employer identification number (EIN) from the contractor. If the independent contractor is unable or unwilling to provide this number, backup withholding is required equal to 31% of payments in excess of the $600 filing threshold. If you do not withhold as required, you as the payer may be held liable for the amount due! In addition, some states now require that businesses report independent contractor contact information in order to help to enforce child support collection efforts. Add this issue to the discussion list for your attorney if you are unsure about your state requirements.

Special Tax Situations

Section 179 First Year Expenses

Small business owners may elect to recover all or part of the cost of certain qualifying property, up to a limit of $125,000 in 2009, by deducting it in the year the property is placed in service. This is the Section 179 deduction. You can elect the Section 179 deduction instead of recovering the cost by taking depreciation deductions over the life of the asset. This amounts to a great benefit to some small business owners since it permits a very large deduction in the first year in which a qualifying asset is purchased and may result in a significantly lower tax bill. Unfortunately, it does not apply to the purchase of personal property that will be put in residential rental property. Therefore it has relatively less value to a rental business owner than to other types of businesses. It does, however, cover personal property used in a rental business which is NOT located in the rental property itself i.e. computer or furniture in your home office. It also covers certain vehicles that are used exclusively in a trade or business. If you purchase personal property that you will use exclusively in your rental business but not in the rental home, you may be eligible for this advantageous tax deduction.

Segmented Depreciation

Another opportunity for tax savings is the benefit derived from more rapidly depreciating certain rental assets by segmenting costs. When a rental property is purchased, it is common to lump the entire purchase price, less the land value, into a single depreciable asset account. The depreciation deduction for this "home" asset is taken over the life of the home, often a lengthy period. An alternative is available to accelerate this deduction by "segmenting" the purchase price into different asset categories. For instance, if you can identify and segregate for depreciation purposes things like carpeting, lighting fixtures, etc. that are not expected to last as long as the home itself, you may take more rapid depreciation on these items, resulting in higher deductions and reduced taxes in the early years. The downside is that this breakdown will not pass IRS scrutiny if it is done haphazardly or arbitrarily, so professional assistance at some cost is usually required. Given this up front investment, it is generally only worthwhile for rental homeowners who have invested significant amounts in purchasing their rental home, say $500,000 or more.

Listed Property

There is one very special category of expenses of which the vacation rental owner should be aware. These are referred to as "Listed Property" since there is a specific list of these type expenditures. The common thread is that they are considered to be high risk for abuse since they have both personal and business applications. These "dual purpose" assets include cars, motorcycles, boats, airplanes, computers, cell phones and electronics. In order to prevent abuse, the IRS mandates special record keeping requirements and depreciation rules. Before you invest money in these type items because of a perceived tax break, you might want to check with your advisor to be certain that you understand what your options are and what is required for deductibility.

Listed property generally includes the following:

◊ Passenger automobiles weighing 6,000 pounds or less.

◊ Any other property used for transportation if the nature of the property lends itself to personal use, such as motorcycles, pick-up trucks, sport utility vehicles, etc.

◊ Any property used for entertainment or recreational purposes (such as photographic, phonographic, communication, and video recording equipment).

◊ Cellular telephones (or other similar telecommunications equipment).

◊ Computers or peripheral equipment.

Listed property does not include:

◊ Photographic, phonographic, communication, or video equipment used exclusively in a taxpayer's trade or business or at the taxpayer's regular business establishment;

◊ Any computer or peripheral equipment used exclusively at a regular business establishment and owned or leased by the person operating the establishment;

◊ An ambulance, hearse, or vehicle used for transporting persons or property for compensation or hire.

◊ Any truck or van placed in service after July 6, 2003 that is a qualified non personal use vehicle.

For purposes of these exceptions, a portion of the taxpayer's home is treated as a regular business establishment only if that portion meets the requirements for deducting expenses attributable to the business use of a home.

Appendix and Online Documents

I have included a number of sample documents, input forms, guest information examples and in-home postings in this appendix that were referenced throughout the book. Online versions of all the referenced pro forma forms and samples shown here may also be found on the web at www.examples.vhallc.com in a WORD format. Although all of these documents are covered by copyright against republication, readers have my unrestricted permission to download, amend and use them for your rental home as desired. You will find the IRS forms and schedules I mentioned in the book on the IRS website at www.IRS.gov. Feel free to amend any of my documents to suit your needs, though I suggest that you do not amend or alter the IRS forms! The documents and forms included are as follows:

Appendix I: Web Input Forms

Appendix II: Sample Rental Documents

Appendix III: Sample In-Home Information

Appendix IV: Sample In-Home Instructions

Appendix V: Sample In-Home Postings

Appendix I

Web Input Forms

The following documents are also available online for your convenience at www.examples.vhallc.com. You may download them and modify them for your use as you see fit. I encourage you to customize them carefully for your home. The more information that you provide to your guests, the better equipped they will be to care for your home and the greater their satisfaction will be with the rental.

◊ **General Information**

◊ **Bulleted Highlights**

◊ **Long Description**

◊ **Short Description**

◊ **Home Layout**

◊ **Home Amenities**

◊ **Specific Area Attractions**

◊ **General Area Activities**

◊ **Seasonal Rental Periods, Minimum Stays and Rates**

General Information

General Information Instructions: Your rental home address and other basic information that you assemble here will be required by every website that you select.

STREET ADDRESS:

CITY:

COUNTY:

STATE:

TYPE OF PROPERTY: (B&B, Home or Condo)

POLICIES:

Sleep Capacity Instructions: (Maximum or Range) This item is used by many web sites to organize their listings and is usually a critical renter consideration. You must provide good and accurate information regarding your sleep capacity to avoid potentially disastrous misunderstandings. Provide a single capacity number or feel free to specify a range if, for instance, you have a sleeper sofa that provides extra capacity.

SLEEP CAPACITY:

_____

_____

_____

Bulleted Highlights

Bulleted Highlights Instructions: Bulleted highlights help renters focus on your best attributes at one glance. Make a list of six to ten of the most appealing things about your home. What is unique about your home? What are the things that will most likely excite interest? What is important in your vacation area?

BULLETED HIGHLIGHTS:

◊

◊

◊

◊

◊

◊

Long Description

Long Description Instructions: A good, detailed description of your rental property can be very powerful and seductive to the potential renter. This is your chance to brag about why you are so proud of your home! In addition, this field is often searched by various search engines. Adding keywords here can be important for renters to find your rental listing.

LONG DESCRIPTION:

_____

_____

_____

_____

_____

_____

_____

_____

_____

_____

Short Description

Short Description Instructions: A carefully worded short description of six to twelve words is often the first thing potential renters see when perusing web rental listings. Cut to the chase and focus on your key property attributes with a distinctive introductory phrase.

SHORT DESCRIPTION:

_____

_____

_____

_____

Home Layout

Home Layout Instructions: The more information that you provide to guests, the more you will increase their confidence and enhance your chances for a rental. While layout is not a common search field, many guests have specific preferences depending on their family or group makeup or anticipated sleeping arrangements.

HOME LAYOUT:

_____

_____

_____

_____

_____

_____

Home Amenities

Home Amenities Instructions: List all that your home has to offer in the way of standard, convenience and luxury features. Listing your home amenities can be very advantageous when potential renters look for specific rental property attributes or compare properties.

HOME AMENITIES:

_____

_____

_____

_____

_____

_____

Specific Area Attractions

Specific Area Attractions Instructions: Many renters use narrow their search to identify listings related to a specific attraction, activity or event in their intended destination area. Be sure to include festivals, sporting events, landmarks and areas of historical interest. It is extremely important to add the proper names of specific area attractions and activities. Hint: Call the Chamber of Commerce for a list of noteworthy area attractions or events.

SPECIFIC AREA ATTRACTIONS:

_____

_____

_____

_____

_____

_____

_____

General Area Activities

General Area Activities Instructions: Be accurate but include everything that you can think of to do in the general area of your vacation rental home. As with other fields, many renters narrow their search by looking for activities and or identifying listings that can satisfy recreational or family preferences.

GENERAL AREA ACTIVITIES:

_____

_____

_____

_____

_____

_____

Seasonal Rental Periods, Minimum Stays and Rates

Instructions: By specifying a minimum stay, you will screen out unwanted inquiries. Minimums can be waived as need be or as open dates approach. For initial rates, start with your prior rates if you have rented previously and consider a small reduction for competitive advantage. Occupancy is imperative early on. You can always raise rates later if your occupancy justifies it.

In Season   (Dates:_____)

                         4 Night Minimum $_____

                         Weekly $_____

Spring   (Dates:_____)

                         Weekly $_____

Summer   (Dates:_____)

                         Weekly $_____

                         Monthly $_____

Fall   (Dates:_____)

                         Weekly $_____

Late Fall   (Dates:_____)

                         Weekly $_____

Holidays:

         Easter Week $_____

         Thanksgiving Week $_____

         Christmas Week $_____

Notes:

         1) Cleaning/linen fee of $_____ is required for all reservations

         2) All rates subject to _____% local and state tax

Appendix II

Sample Rental Documents

The following documents are also available online for your convenience at www.examples.vhallc.com. You may download them and modify them for your use as you see fit. I encourage you to customize them carefully for your home. The more information that you provide to your guests, the better equipped they will be to care for your home and the greater their satisfaction will be with the rental.

Since these are the primary documents that will define your rental relationships, I urge you to discuss them with trusted advisors once they are complete. Every circumstance is different and these samples are not meant to cover all situations.

◊ **Sample Introduction Letter**
◊ **Sample Guest License Agreement**
◊ **Sample Directions**
◊ **Sample Home Access Detail**
◊ **Sample Driver Name Request**
◊ **Sample Credentials**

Sample Introduction Letter

Dear Guest:

Thank you for considering my home for your vacation stay. It is a first class property and I very much want your repeat business, so I work hard to make sure you are happy with your decision and satisfied with the accommodations. There is no wrong time to call.

My Credentials: The first order of business is to provide you assurance of my legitimacy so that you are comfortable in mailing your payment. I am an attorney in Florida, Georgia and South Carolina. I have attached my credentials, including my professional license numbers, plus references. You may pull up the web sites of the respective licensing bodies and search by license number for verification of my good standing. I am sure you are familiar generally with what it takes to obtain these credentials and understand how zealously I protect my standing, clean record and good name. The professional references listed are also my good friends. You may certainly call any of them as you desire, but I would generally rather that they not be bothered any more than necessary for obvious reasons. I'm sure you understand.

Lease Agreement: I have attached a lease agreement for your signature. This is an industry standard document but please read it carefully. This signed agreement must be received with your deposit check in order to lock in your reservation. Please feel free to email me with questions; however, no modifications are permitted to the lease document.

Payment Requirements: Payment requirements and refund policies are spelled out in detail in the lease agreement, but please do not hesitate to contact me if you have questions. All reservations are confirmed with a 50% advance payment due upon booking. Reservations will be canceled if advance payment is not received within seven (7) days of booking. Balance of rent is due 30 days prior to check-in. The above policies protect both of us by allowing your early reservation with less than full payment and preventing my property from sitting not rented due to payment issues. The rapid deposit payment requirements are necessary because I take the home off of the rental market based on your initial reservation. I suggest second day delivery mail just to be on the safe side but that is up to you. The delivery address is [*insert delivery address here*]. Please do not request signature on delivery as I am in and out and I will call if payment doesn't arrive.

Logistical Arrangements: Please remember that four-wheel drive or chains are required for winter access. You should simply proceed to the home and use the access key code *[insert code here]* on the lock boxes on either of the front doors (upper or lower). The same code works for both lock boxes. Record this code prominently in your travel items. In the unlikely event that the parking chain is locked, keys to the chain locks are also included in the lock boxes. I have attached directions to the home, but please email or call if you have any questions. The phone number of *[insert property address here]* is *[insert number here]*.

Trip Cancellation: Please obtain trip interruption insurance as you may desire (www.insuremytrip.com) since payments are not refundable for weather related reasons.

Property Information: The home is fully equipped with dishes, flatware, glasses, sheets, towels and linens to accommodate the maximum occupancy. There is of course a washer and dryer. A starter supply only of paper towels, toilet tissue, soap, trash bags and dishwashing detergent is provided. You will need laundry detergent. You can bring additional supplies with you or wait until after you arrive to purchase these items. Cribs, high chairs and strollers are available through Smith Rentals (000-000-0000). I suggest Highland Chalet Rentals (000-000-0000) for off slope discounts on equipment rentals and lift tickets.

I hope this information is enough to get things going. Thank you for being my guest and please do not hesitate to email requests for additional information. I look forward to your visit.

Thank you,

[Insert Your Name Here]

ATTACHED:

> Lease Agreement
>
> Directions
>
> Credentials (Optional)

Sample Guest License Agreement

Address: *[Insert Your Property Address]*

Arrival Date: _____ Departure Date:_____

1. This home is privately owned, including furnishings. Guest(s) acknowledges that (s)he is a licensee of the owner and not a tenant, and is not acquiring any interest in the property. Guest(s) agrees to compensate Owner for any excessive cleaning, any damages or missing items upon departure.

2. Owner is not responsible for any damages or injury which may occur at the premises, nor responsible for any articles lost or stolen, or left on the premises.

3. Occupancy and use of premises shall not be such as to disturb or offend neighbors. Owner reserves the right to terminate this agreement and ask disruptive guests to vacate premises with no refund.

4. Guests(s) agree Owner or Owner's agents may enter premises to make repairs or maintenance, or for other necessary purposes. All reasonable efforts will be made to handle maintenance emergencies; however, no guarantee can be made that such problems can be resolved immediately.

5. **Pets are not permitted under any circumstances.** If this provision is violated, Owner reserves the right to terminate this agreement, require the Guest(s) to vacate premises with no refund and charge for de-fleaing.

6. Check-in time is 4:00 PM or later. Check out time is 10:00 AM or earlier. **There is a $25.00 per hour charge for late checkout**. There will be no refund for early departure.

7. **Payment and Refund Policy**:

    a. **Reservations made > 30 days out:** All reservations are confirmed with a 50% advance payment due upon booking. Reservations will be canceled if advance payment is not received within seven (7) days of booking; therefore, first or second day expedited delivery is strongly suggested. Balance of rent is due 30 days prior to check-in. **Reservation will be cancelled <u>with no refund</u> if balance of rent is not received <u>at least</u> 30 days prior to check-in.** Reservations must be cancelled within seven (7) days of booking to receive a full refund. Any cancellation occurring after seven (7) days of booking will forfeit the 50% advance payment unless the property is rebooked and confirmed. If the property is rebooked and confirmed, advance payment will be refunded less a $250 cancellation fee. Refunds, if any, will be mailed after the original rental period is complete. Changing a reservation in any way constitutes a cancellation and the same terms apply. There is no refund for inclement or undesirable weather, including hurricane evacuation. **Visit insuremytrip.com for trip interruption insurance and indicate by initialing that you understand this option:** _____

b. **Reservations made < 30 days out:** If you reserve a time period less than 30 days out, full payment is due immediately by overnight mail and reservations will be canceled if advance payment is not received within five (5) days of booking. If you book within five (5) days of your arrival, payment is due immediately by overnight mail and must be received no later than your day of arrival or reservations will be cancelled.

8. Guest acknowledges this reservation is only for the number of adults and children listed. Number _____.

I have read, understand and accept the terms of this agreement,

Print name:_____

Telephone:_____

Email:_____

Signature:_____

Date of Booking:_____

Address:_____

Rent	$_____	
Tax	_____	
Cleaning	_____	
Total	$_____	
Advance	$_____	50% Due Now
Balance	$_____	Due by _____

Sample Directions

Directions to [*Insert Property Address Here*] from [*Insert Major City Here*]

◊   Begin at Hwy. 000 South at US 000 (at Wendys) or US 000 (left turn)
◊   Follow Hwy. 000 South
◊   12.8 miles to   [*Note: Lowes, best food store, and closest liquor store is on left before you get to Hwy. 000]*
◊   Hwy. 000 North (at Texaco)
◊   Turn right
◊   4.2 miles to *[Note: If you missed Lowes Foods, Food Lion is on right along here]*
◊   "T" intersection
◊   Turn left
◊   One half mile to Hwy. 000 North
◊   Road splits, stay right, staying on Hwy. 000 North
◊   3.6 miles up mountain to Town of Cold Mountain
◊   As soon as you get to the top of the hill, you will see windmill on left.
◊   Turn left up hill <u>between</u> Real Estate building and the town hall/police station/sledding area (both on your left).
◊   Proceed up steep hill,
◊   Rental home is on left near top (brown house)

Code lock on door: [*insert code here*]:   open lock to retrieve door key

Call my cell at [*insert number here*] if you have a problem – I always have this phone with me.

The police department is very helpful if you have any difficulties or emergency situations. Their non-emergency number is [*insert number here*].

Thank you,

[*Insert Your Name Here*]

Sample Home Access Detail

A pass for each guest vehicle will be called in to the security gate prior to your arrival based on the Drivers List information you return to me. As for directions, www.mapquest.com is generally quite accurate but please give it a try and let me know early if you are unsure of anything. When you arrive at the gate, you will give the attendant the house address and the driver's name and will be given vehicle passes for the rental period. This does not mean that other licensed drivers can't drive during the visit, but only that initially someone has to identify themselves at the gate and get a pass for each automobile.

The driveway can accommodate only three small to medium vehicles maximum. Please arrange to park additional vehicles across the street or in the reception center lot. Street parking is not permitted due to requirements for fire truck access, with the exception of the cul-de-sac for short periods. Parking on the street in the cul-de-sac is not considered to be an impediment to fire trucks, but I am unsure if there is still a risk of towing.

Access to the house is by a code lock hanging from the front door handle. You will notice a digital readout on the handle itself. The door code for your visit will be [*insert code here*]. Punch in the code and the key assembly will drop into your hand. After unlocking the door, please return the key assembly to the code lock. You may continue to utilize the door code or use the key supplied inside the home for the duration of your stay

If you have any problems with getting in, call me at [*insert number here*] or call [*insert alternate contact*] at [*insert number here*] as we have a backup access plan in place.

[*Insert Your Name Here*]

Sample Driver Name Request

Submission of this form does not mean that other licensed drivers can't drive during the visit, but initially someone has to identify themselves at the gate and get a pass for each automobile. Please identify one driver per car to accept this initial responsibility.

Driver Name /Car #1_____

Driver Name/Car #2 _____

Driver Name/Car #3 _____

Note: The driveway can accommodate only three vehicles. Please arrange to park additional vehicles across the street or in the reception center lot. Street parking is not permitted due to requirements for fire truck access.

Driver #4 _____

Driver #5 _____

Driver #6 _____

Please return this information with your final payment.

Sample Credentials

Home or Business Addresses
[Insert Mailing Addresses]

Web Addresses
[Insert Web Addresses]

Education /Certification
[Insert Education /Certifications]

Affiliations and Accreditations
[Insert Affiliations and Accreditations]

Organizations and Clubs
[Insert Affiliations and Accreditations]
[Insert Picture Here]
[Insert Name]

Telephone Contact Information
[Insert telephone or other information as Desired]

Appendix III

Sample In-Home Information

The following documents are also available online for your convenience at www.examples.vhallc.com. You may download them and modify them for your use as you see fit. I encourage you to customize them carefully for your home. The more information that you provide to your guests, the better equipped they will be to care for your home and the greater their satisfaction will be with the rental.

◊ **Sample General Home Information**
◊ **Sample Area Restaurant Information**
◊ **Sample Area Activities Information**

Sample General Home Information

WELCOME TO OUR COMMUNITY AND THE CAROLINA COAST! I would be honored if you would consider my home to be your home at the beach.

For critical or emergency maintenance issues, call [*insert contact*] **at** [*insert telephone number*]. If you cannot get in touch with him, backup emergency maintenance is available by calling [*insert backup name*] at [*insert backup number*]. Please email me at [*insert email address*] for routine maintenance requests or suggested improvements. For additional housekeeping service, feel free to call [*insert housekeeper name*] at [*insert housekeeper number*] to make your own arrangements. Certain locked storage areas are designated as owners' closets and unavailable to guests. If you discover that there are any items missing or broken which are available for under $30, feel free to replace at Target and send me the receipt for prompt reimbursement. Coolers are stored under the kitchen bar for your use. Do not be concerned with watering the three indoor plants as the housekeeper will do this on Saturday. The shower lights are on timers to prevent overheating. Be aware (not afraid) of alligator in lagoon!

Please use garbage bags and place trash in outside cans. Make sure cans are secured so raccoons will not get in them.

- Garbage pickup for is Tuesday, with additional collection on Friday between Memorial Day and Labor Day.
- For recycling information, please contact Public Works at [*insert #*].
- You should expect the pest control service to call before coming. I treat both outside and inside and the occasional dead or dying bug means it's working.

Please do not set air conditioning thermostats below 68 degrees, as they do not operate efficiently at lower temperatures. If you elect to leave windows and doors open to enjoy the breeze, please make certain that the central air system is turned off. Also, please do not adjust refrigerator or freezer controls as they must be allowed time to cool down after placing food in them.

I think of my guests as family and hope you return to visit again in the future!

Sample Area Restaurant Information

The following restaurants are within a short drive of the home.

Beech Mountain:

Brick Oven Pasta & Pizzeria / across from town hall / 387-4209 (good food and great beer selection)

Frazier's Steakhouse & Nightclub / at the entrance of Ski Beech / 387-4171

Fred's Backside Deli / behind Fred's Mercantile Store / 387-9331 (good breakfast)

Jackalope's View / at Archer's Mountain Inn halfway down the mountain toward Banner Elk 898-9004 (very good formal dining)

Beech Haven Restaurant / bottom of mountain toward Banner Elk / 898-9484 (good breakfast and country buffet for lunch only)

Los Arcoiris / bottom of mountain toward Banner Elk / 898-4123 (excellent Mexican food)

Banner Elk:

Louisiana Purchase / Main Street / 963-5087 (see review below)

Mike's Inland Seafood / other side of Banner Elk / 265-1611 (excellent Calabash style seafood)

Linville:

Eseeola Lodge / May through November 6:45 till 8:30 PM

Thursday night seafood buffet is spectacular / Coat and Tie required

Blowing Rock:

Best Cellar / behind Food Lion on Hwy 321 Bypass / 295-3466 (excellent!)

Crippen's Country Inn & Restaurant / 239 Sunset Drive / 295-3487

Twigs / beside ABC store on Hwy 321 Bypass / 295-5050

Sample Area Activities Information

The listed activities are available in the surrounding area:

The Beech Mountain Chamber of Commerce (www.beechmtn.com) would probably be a good source of information on local activities and give you a pretty good idea of what to expect in the way of weather during your visit. Also check www.fredsgeneral.com for local weather and other info. You never know what you will see in the way of wildlife and hiking is always a fun and healthy option. Banner Elk is at the bottom of the mountain (www.bannerelk.org) with lots to see and do. Grandfather Mountain (www.grandfather.com) is the one in the distance you can see from my deck (about 15 minutes), and the Blue Ridge Parkway is a beautiful drive. Check out Tweetsie Railroads website (www.tweetsie.com)to make sure that they are open - kids like that - and I feel sure they would be. Shopping is neat in Blowing Rock (www.blowingrock.com) (unique stores, ice cream shoppes, etc.) and there are some excellent restaurants in the area (www.blowingrock.org/dining.html) (I have notes on many of them at the house). There is also the original Mast General Store (www.mastgeneralstore.com) that is quite an interesting little side trip. Check out Country Retreat Family Billiards - first class and family atmosphere with video arcade, widescreen TVs (888-963-6260) in Foscoe and the home of some nationally ranked young pool players. They don't have a website but are listed on a number of related sites – try searching on their name to see what I mean. Also, call the Beech Mountain Club (www.beechmtnclub.org) to inquire about activities on their calendar (888-387-4208 Ext. 222). You are eligible to use their facilities as a guest at my home since I am a member. There is a very nice little horseback riding farm nearby suitable for children if they are open (Smith Quarter Horse Farm 888-898-4932) and for more experienced riders there is Blowing Rock Farm in Blowing Rock for access to Cone Park (www.mountaintimes.com/summer/mosescone.php3), which I have not done but would love to. I have LOTS of games and movies for down periods just in case. All the above websites have links which give you some idea of the fun and diversity to be found in the area. Hope this helps you to plan your trip!

Thanks again for visiting and please come back!

Appendix IV

Sample In-Home Instructions

The following documents are also available online for your convenience at www.examples.vchallc.com. You may download them and modify them for your use as you see fit. I encourage you to customize them carefully for your home. The more information that you provide to your guests, the better equipped they will be to care for your home and the greater their satisfaction will be with the rental.

◊ **Sample Fire Prevention Instructions**
◊ **Sample Departure Instructions**
◊ **Sample Grill Instructions**
◊ **Sample Fireplace Instructions**
◊ **Sample Propane Instructions**

Sample Fire Prevention Instructions

<u>The island is susceptible to fire due to constant winds, natural habitat and dry conditions.</u> The following information is for your safety and peace of mind. Fire extinguishers are located on the pantry wall in the kitchen and in the closet of the upstairs master. All members of the family should be familiar with their location. Water hoses are hooked up at both ends of the house. Candles are not permitted in this home. Although this is a non-smoking home, I have provided ashtrays in the top corner kitchen cabinet if smokers elect to smoke outside. Please strongly discourage guests from tossing butts into the pine straw. It is thought that careless disposal of cigarettes is how two local residents lost their homes right down the beach from here. Thank you for your assistance in keeping our community safe.

Thanks again for visiting and please come back!

Sample Departure Instructions

Please leave the home in good condition. **DEPARTURE TIME IS 10:00 AM.** <u>Please respect this time in order to allow our housekeeping staff sufficient time to prepare for incoming guests.</u> *This is critical.*

Upon departure, please leave the home in reasonably tidy order. Please do not rearrange furniture or move furnishings outdoors. Keys and pool passes should be left as found. Lock windows and doors and place garbage in outdoor containers. Do not lock the deadbolt on the front door, just the handle code lock as you found it when you arrived.

Please do not leave dirty utensils in the home. You may of course wash them and leave them on the counter to dry or fill and run the dishwasher. On some occasions when I have no one arriving immediately, I allow the housekeeper flexibility in her cleaning schedule. Therefore, it may be several days before she arrives to clean and we wouldn't want to have dirty dishes sitting around to attract varmints!

Thanks again for visiting and please come back!

Sample Grill Instructions

Always work with lid open. It is not necessary to use lava rocks or briquettes with heat deflectors. Gas control knobs on side of grill should be off. Cut on gas at propane tank. Follow directions on grill. When finished, cut off gas at control knobs and at tank. Please leave soiled tools in the sink when you leave or clean tools hanging on the cupboard. Note: If fireplace stays at low heat, see vapor lock comments in Grill Book in kitchen drawer.

Thanks again for visiting and please come back!

Sample Fireplace Instructions

This fireplace is designed to run cleanly with damper closed. However, you may want to slightly crack door or window occasionally.

Lighting Instructions:

<u>When pilot off</u> - Gas control knob on right front bottom of fireplace logs should be off. Cut on gas at propane tank and at red cutoff switch on porch. Cut on log gas control knob to "pilot" and light gas using electronic ignition button on left front bottom of logs.

<u>When pilot on</u> – Simply turn log gas control knob from pilot setting to heat setting desired.

"High" heat setting will run through your gas in a day (or less) if run continuously but does produce good heat, particularly after the hearth warms up. A full tank should last considerably longer at "low" setting and when run intermittently. When finished, cut off gas only at log gas control knob if you wish to leave the pilot light on. Depending on your expected usage, you may elect to turn the pilot off by cutting off the valve at tank and at red cutoff switch, both on porch.

Thanks again for visiting and please come back!

Sample Propane Instructions

Both the grill and fireplace use propane. They are provided for your enjoyment as weather permits with the understanding that guests are responsible for providing their own fuel. There is usually some propane in the tanks but <u>providing propane must be the responsibility of the renter</u>. If you want to use either the grill or the fireplace, I suggest that you make sure the spare tank is full in case the connected tank runs dry. There is nothing more frustrating than having your food half-done or sitting in front of a nice fire and the gas running out. Remember that propane tank fittings <u>unscrew in a clockwise direction</u>! You can switch out empties for full tanks for a modest cost at Island Hardware, the Piggly Wiggly or Lowes in Mt. Olive.

<u>IN ANY CASE, KEEP EMPTY OR FULL PROPANE TANKS OUTSIDE THE HOUSE AT ALL TIMES.</u>

Thanks again for visiting and please come back!

Appendix V

Sample In-Home Postings

The following documents are also available online for your convenience at www.examples.vhallc.com. You may download them and modify them for your use as you see fit. I encourage you to customize them carefully for your home. The more information that you provide to your guests, the better equipped they will be to care for your home and the greater their satisfaction will be with the rental.

◊ **Sample Telephone Numbers**
◊ **Sample Clean Filters Posting**
◊ **Sample Electrical Panel Layout**
◊ **Sample No Smoking Posting**
◊ **Sample Grill Posting**
◊ **Sample Fireplace Posting**
◊ **Sample Propane Posting**

Telephone Numbers

Emergency	911	
Community Gate House	888-2128	(Call for passes)
Back Gate	888-2114	

GOLF

Land Course	888-2301	(Tough!)
Links Course	888-2180	(Fun and Expensive)
Patriots Challenge	888-0042	(Best Value!)
Wild West	858-9000	(Easier but wet)
Savannah National	888-7799	
Sugar Hill	218-3777	(Tough and New)

RESTAURANTS

Boat Ramp Restaurant	888-8000	(On Inlet)
Station 11	888-3355	(O'Leary's Island)
Franks Restaurant	728-3474	(Downtown)
Penny's Grill	728-2345	(Great!)

SPAS

Nova Spa	888-3838
Dunes Spa	888-2555
Nearly Paradise	888-6827
Studio 99 Yoga and Massage	389-2488

SERVICES

Bike Rentals	888-2293
Beach Chair Rentals	678-1009

Filters Posting

<u>Please clean the filters</u> in both the clothes dryer and hand held vacuum before and after every use.

Electrical Service Panel Layout

(Breaker Labels with Amps)

Left Side Panel	**Right Side Panel**
1. Heat s/50	2. Heat s/ 50
3. Heat s/50	4. Heat s/50
5. Air Conditioning s/40	6. Range s/50
7. Air Conditioning s/40	8. Range s/50
9. Water Heater s/30	10. Air Conditioning s/40
11. Water Heater s/30	12. Air Conditioning s/40
13. Second Floor Master Bath 20	14. Dryer s/30
14. Downstairs Bath/20	16. Dryer s/30
15. Dishwasher/20	18. Second Floor Hall Bath 20
19. Sink Light and Disposal 20	20. 2nd and 3rd Floor Bedrooms 15
21. Downstairs Bedroom 15	22. Kitchen Receptacles 20
23. Living Room 15	24. Kitchen Receptacles 20
25. 2nd Floor Master Bedroom 15	26. Microwave Oven 20
26. 27. Bathroom and O/S Rec 15	28. Refrigerator 20
29. Kitchen and Dining Room 15	30. Washer 20

Smoking Policy

<u>Please do not smoke inside the home</u>. Renters are accountable for burn holes and stains. Ashtrays have been provided for those who wish to smoke on the deck or porch. Please see in-home instructions regarding fire prevention. Thank you for your help.

Grill Posting

<u>Always work with the grill lid open.</u> It is not necessary to use lava rocks or briquettes with this type grill. Gas control knobs on the side of the grill should be off. Cut on gas at propane tank. Follow directions on grill. When finished, cut off gas at control knobs and at tank. Please leave soiled tools in the sink when you leave or clean tools hanging on the cupboard.

Note: If fireplace stays at low heat and does not properly heat for grilling, see vapor lock comments in grill instruction book located in the kitchen drawer.

Fireplace Posting

This gas fireplace is designed to run cleanly with the damper closed. However, you may want to slightly crack door or window occasionally to ensure the highest air quality in the home.

Lighting Instructions:

When pilot off - Gas control knob on right front bottom of fireplace logs should be off. Cut on gas at propane tank and at red cutoff switch on porch. Cut on log gas control knob to "pilot" and light gas using electronic ignition button on left front bottom of logs.

When pilot on – Simply turn log gas control knob from pilot setting to heat setting desired. "High" heat setting will run through your gas in a day (or less) if run continuously but does produce good heat, particularly after the hearth warms up. A full tank should last considerably longer at "low" setting and when run intermittently. When finished, cut off gas only at log gas control knob if you wish to leave the pilot light on. Depending on your expected usage, you may elect to turn the pilot off by cutting off the valve at tank and at red cutoff switch, both on porch.

Propane Posting

Please help me to continue to make a grill available for all rental guests. The cost, availability and procurement of propane are the responsibility of the renter. See in-home instructions for nearby propane retailers. **Caution:** Do not keep empty or full tanks <u>inside</u> the house at all - always leave on decks.

Index

CPSIA information can be obtained at www.ICGtesting.com
Printed in the USA
LVOW050940120412

277284LV00004B/146/P